About the Author

Liz Palika has been teaching dogs and their owners in Northern San Diego County for almost twenty-five years. Her training is based on an understanding of dogs and what makes them tick. There is no funny stuff but lots of common sense.

Liz is also the author of more than forty-five books; her dog-training book, *All Dogs Need Some Training,* was listed by *Pet Life* magazine as one of the ten best dog-training books available to dog owners. Liz's books have been honored with several awards from Dog Writers Association of America, Cat Writers' Association, ASPCA, Purina, and San Diego Book Writers. In 2005, she was awarded a Distinguished Service award from Dog Writers Association of America.

A former member of the National Association of Dog Obedience Instructors and founding member of the Association of Pet Dog Trainers (APDT), Liz is also a charter member of the International Association of Canine Professionals and is a Certified Dog Trainer (CDT) through this organization. She is also a member of the International Association of Animal Behavior Consultants, and an AKC Canine Good Citizen Evaluator.

About Howell Book House

Since 1961, Howell Book House has been America's premier publisher of pet books. We're dedicated to companion animals and the people who love them, and our books reflect that commitment. Our stable of authors—training experts, veterinarians, breeders, and other authorities—is second to none. And we've won more Maxwell Awards from the Dog Writers Association of America than any other publisher.

As we head toward the half-century mark, we're more committed than ever to providing new and innovative books, along with the classics our readers have grown to love. From bringing home a new puppy to competing in advanced equestrian events, Howell has the titles that keep animal lovers coming back again and again.

Contents

Shopping List

You'll need to do a bit of stocking-up before you bring your new dog or puppy home. Below is a basic list of some must-have supplies. For more detailed information on the selection of each item below, consult Chapter 5. For specific guidance on what grooming tools you'll need, review Chapter 7.

☐ Food dish   ☐ Nail clippers (scissors type for large dogs)

☐ Water dish   ☐ Grooming tools

☐ Dog food   ☐ Chew toys (heavy duty; for large dogs)

☐ Leash   ☐ Toys

☐ Collar   ☐ ID tag

☐ Crate

There are likely to be a few other items that you're dying to pick up before bringing your dog home. Use the following blanks to note any additional items you'll be shopping for.

☐ _____

☐ _____

☐ _____

☐ _____

☐ _____

☐ _____

☐ _____

☐ _____

☐ _____

☐ _____

☐ _____

☐ _____

Pet Sitter's Guide

We can be reached at (___)_____-_____ Cell phone (___)_____-_____

_____

We will return on _____ (date) at _____ (approximate time)

Dog's Name _____

Breed, Age, and Sex _____

Important Names and Numbers

Vet's Name _____ Phone (___)_____- _____

Address_____

Emergency Vet's Name _____ Phone (___)_____- _____

Address_____

Poison Control _____ (or call vet first)

Other individual to contact in case of emergency (someone the dog knows well and will respond to) to contact in case of emergency or in case the dog is being protective and will not allow the pet sitter in _____

_____

Care Instructions

In the following three blanks let the sitter know what to feed, how much, and when; when the dog should go out; when to give treats; and when to exercise the dog.

Morning_____

_____

Afternoon _____

_____

Evening _____

_____

Medications needed (dosage and schedule) _____

_____

Any special medical conditions _____

_____

Grooming instructions _____

_____

My dog's favorite playtime activities, quirks, and other tips_____

_____

_____

Part I
The World of the Labrador Retriever

The Labrador Retriever

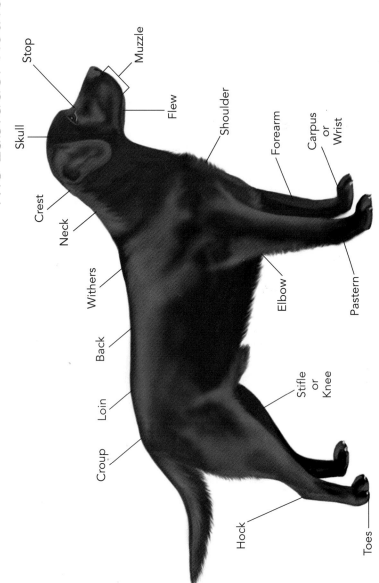

- Stop
- Skull
- Crest
- Neck
- Withers
- Back
- Loin
- Croup
- Muzzle
- Flew
- Shoulder
- Forearm
- Carpus or Wrist
- Elbow
- Pastern
- Stifle or Knee
- Hock
- Toes

Chapter 1

What Is a Labrador Retriever?

A Labrador Retriever puppy is a bouncy bundle of black, yellow, or chocolate fun and energy. Versatility is the breed's middle name. A Lab might be a guide dog, an assistance dog, a hunting companion, a therapy dog, or work in law enforcement.

If you decide to show your dogs in conformation or to compete in obedience or field trials, once again, Labs are a very popular choice. Because of their happy-go-lucky attitude, Labs are great with children and adults. When it's time for your family to choose a pet, you probably can't go wrong with a Labrador Retriever if you are an active family on the go and want a dog who will be on the go, too. A Lab is never happier than when he's with his family or his person.

The Sporting Breeds

The Labrador Retriever is a sporting dog, as classified by the American Kennel Club and other breed registries. The Sporting Group includes the other retrievers, such as the Golden Retriever and the Chesapeake Bay Retriever, as well as the setters, spaniels, and pointers. The breeds that make up the Sporting Group were all bred to work alongside and help out hunters.

Their hunting skills varied according to the purpose for which they were bred. But most of the dogs in the Sporting Group have some characteristics in common. First of all, they are intelligent and quick to learn. Training is easy when you have learned how to motivate the dog. But these dogs can also think for themselves, and when they do, training can be a challenge.

Labrador Retrievers are sporting dogs. If you never hunt with your dog, you'll have to find other ways to keep him active.

Sporting dogs are also athletic and busy, especially as puppies. They need daily exercise and activities. Without enough exercise and an occupation to keep them busy, these dogs can get into trouble.

The Lab's Physical Appearance

The Labrador Retriever should be medium in size and give the appearance of a dog who is strong, muscular, and active. He is well balanced, not clumsy or spindly. He should appear ready for action at any time. There is a distinct difference between the sexes. Male Labs should look masculine: strong, thick-necked, and with heavier bones. Females are definitely more feminine: strong and athletic yet not as heavily boned as the males or as muscled. In this section, I briefly describe the ideal Labrador Retriever based on the breed standard.

The Head

When looking at a Lab, the first thing you notice is the dog's head. The Lab has a fairly broad skull. The head should not have big, heavy, apple cheeks or flews (lips) that are too pendulous. The head should have a neat, clean appearance. The muzzle should be strong and never thin or pointed.

The eyes are where we see that irresistible sweet, kind, alert expression. The eyes should be the shape of a rounded diamond. Although some roundness in the eyes can be attractive, they should not resemble the round eyes of a Cocker Spaniel,

The Labrador Retriever has a broad, strong skull. The head is a striking feature of the breed.

nor should they be too almond-shaped. They should be a warm brown on all dogs, no matter what the coat color, and maybe a bit darker on a yellow Lab. When you look into a Lab's eyes, you should see instant friendliness.

The ears should be set off the side of the skull, not too high and not too low. They should be of medium size, hanging so that the bottom tips are about two inches below the eyes. The ears should not be so big or so small that they draw attention to themselves. And they should never be long or folded, as they are on many hounds.

The Body

The neck is strong and of medium length. There is nothing elegant about this dog. He should remind you of a small Mack truck—agile but strong and sturdy. He should appear well balanced, with all parts of him in proportion and working together correctly.

As you continue down the neck, past the withers (point of the shoulder), the topline (along the spine) should be rather level, never swayback or sloping. The chest should be deep with ribs like a barrel. The front legs are well underneath the dog, allowing a prominent breastbone to show and creating the picture of a powerful chest.

What Is a Breed Standard?

A breed standard is a detailed description of the perfect dog of that breed. Breeders use the standard as a guide in their breeding programs, and judges use it to evaluate the dogs in conformation shows. The standard is written by the national breed club, using guidelines established by the registry that recognizes the breed (such as the AKC or UKC).

The first section of the breed standard gives a brief overview of the breed's history. Then it describes the dog's general appearance and size as an adult. Next is a detailed description of the head and neck, then the back and body, and the front and rear legs. The standard then describes the ideal coat and how the dog should be presented in the show ring. It also lists all acceptable colors, patterns, and markings. Then there's a section on how the dog moves, called *gait*. Finally, there's a general description of the dog's temperament.

Each section also lists characteristics that are considered to be faults or disqualifications in the conformation ring. Superficial faults in appearance are often what distinguish a pet-quality dog from a show- or competition-quality dog. However, some faults affect the way a dog moves or his overall health. And faults in temperament are serious business.

You can read all the AKC breed standards at www.akc.org.

All four legs should have good, thick bone, with the front legs coming straight down from the shoulders. The rear legs should be well bent at the knee or stifle. The hindquarters should be thick, with well-muscled thighs.

As a Labrador Retriever moves, his tail usually wags happily from side to side. It should never be carried curled up over the back like a hound's tail. A tail that is carried too low or between the legs will give the appearance of timidity.

The Lab's tail is called an otter tail because it's thick at the base and tapers down to a tip, like the tail of an otter. The tail should be well covered with a very distinctive short, dense coat. The underside of the tail should never have any long, feathery hair on it.

Labs come in black, yellow, and chocolate.

The Coat and Colors

The Labrador Retriever comes in three solid colors: black, yellow, and chocolate. The black is very black; the yellow ranges from an almost white to a dark yellow; and the chocolate is a rich brown. A white spot on the chest is permissible.

Dogs in all colors should have a waterproof, double coat. The thick undercoat lies beneath the topcoat. The topcoat should be a bit rough to the touch and doesn't have to lie flat. In fact, if the coat is too slick, the dog probably doesn't have a good undercoat and would not be useful as a retriever in cold water. The undercoat acts as insulation and, working in conjunction with the coat's natural oil, helps repel water.

> **TIP**
>
> All three colors are equal in the Labrador Retriever. A yellow Lab is the same breed as a chocolate Lab and a black Lab.

The Lab's Character

Labrador Retrievers have been the most popular dog in America for many years, for several reasons. The breed's size and easy-care coat certainly have something to do with this popularity, but most enthusiasts say they love the dogs' personality.

Labs are fun. They love to play and are always up for whatever you want to do. You like hiking? Labs love to go for a hike! You like to go swimming? They'll do that, too. Labs chase balls and catch Frisbees. They will play with the kids, and go jogging with Dad. Labs enjoy life!

Family and Friends

Labrador Retrievers are devoted family dogs. They love everyone in the family equally with loyalty and devotion. When you come home, even if you've only been gone a few minutes, you'll be greeted with a wagging tail, a wriggling body, and a smiling face.

This breed is also very devoted to his friends. Once you're a friend, you will be greeted with enthusiasm each and every time the dog sees you, no matter whether it's weekly or once a year.

Intelligence and Trainability

Labs are bright dogs. They are smart enough to get into trouble and can figure out problems: Many Labs have figured out how to open sliding glass doors to let themselves into the house! The breed is also very trainable. When you have figured out how to motivate the dog and keep his attention, Labs can (and have) been trained in agility, flyball, obedience, therapy dog work, search and rescue, and much more.

Although Lab puppies can be very silly and easily distracted, once past adolescence they can become more serious about training. Puppy owners just need to be patient and consistent with training.

Active Dogs

Labs do best in a household where the people want to do things with him. If they're left alone for too many hours each day, many Labs will find ways to amuse themselves, and often those activities will be unwelcome. Labs have been known to bark too much, dig holes in the lawn, pull down the woodpile searching for critters, and escape from the yard. Labs can also be destructive chewers. However, when you can spend time with him every day and can make sure the dog gets enough exercise, your Lab will be a wonderful companion dog.

Not Protective

If you're looking for a protective dog, perhaps a dog who would give his life to defend you, don't get a Lab. Labs will bark a few times when someone approaches the house, but other than that, the breed is not at all protective. This breed was bred to be nonthreatening.

This trait is one of the reasons why they are such good family dogs. Not only are Labs always ready to play, but they also don't get upset when other people play. For example, if your son brings home his friends and the kids begin wrestling in the backyard, the Lab may either join in or just watch. A protective dog will be very upset. To a protective dog, wrestling is a potential attack. But not to a Lab.

Working Dog Extraordinaire

Several of the breed's characteristics have made them very popular as working dogs. The Lab's keen sense of smell and love of play has lead many military and law enforcement agencies to use them for detection work. With a play session as a reward, Labs will search for drugs, contraband, and other items. They are also excellent search and rescue dogs.

The breed's devotion to his owners and trainability have made it popular as assistance and service dogs. The Lab's wonderful temperament and friendliness lead them to be wonderful therapy dogs. Labrador Retrievers can be found working in many different occupations.

Because Labs are smart and active and easily trained, they have become popular as working dogs.

Chapter 2

The Labrador Retriever Yesterday and Today

There are many theories about the origin of the breed known today as the Labrador Retriever. One point on which all historians seem to agree is that the breed originally came from Newfoundland in far northeastern Canada, not Labrador. They were known by several names—including the St. John's Water Dog, the Little Newfoundlander, and the Black Water Dog.

Some believe the Labrador Retriever was developed by the fishermen off the coast of Newfoundland, and that the breed was the result of an attempt to produce a somewhat smaller dog because the Newfoundland breed is a bit cumbersome. The dog had to be a good retriever, had to have good bone and strong limbs to pull heavy loads, and needed a dense coat thick enough to withstand the cold water, but one that would not ball up with ice. She had to be eager to please, able to swim great distances, and happy to live on a diet of fish and whatever else could be scrounged up. The Labrador Retriever became that dog. But how?

That is the mystery. Some believe the large Newfoundland dogs were indigenous to Newfoundland. Others believe there were no dogs there until the Europeans came to the coast to fish.

It appears that the native inhabitants of the island, the Beothucks, did not have any dogs. The British began to fish in Newfoundland in 1498, and about twenty years later they built some settlements. Most of the settlers were hunters as well as fishermen. They wanted dogs to hunt and retrieve their fish and work around the settlement. Most historians of the breed agree that the fishing boats commonly ran between Newfoundland and Poole Harbour, in Dorset. The fishermen went back and forth to sell their salted codfish, and their dogs often made the trip as well.

The dogs brought by the settlers were probably the only dogs in Newfoundland, and over the centuries they were bred and trained to meet the needs of their owners. From these various breeds of dogs, bred over a period of 280 years under rigorous conditions, the Newfoundland dog and the Labrador Retriever were developed. They were the product of their environment and survival of the fittest and, perhaps, selective breeding.

Some time around 1818, some of these dogs were seen and purchased in England. The English waterfowl hunters were quick to appreciate these talented dogs. The Second Earl of Malmesbury was said to have purchased several from some of the fishing boat captains, and, liking these dogs, he continued to import and breed them. Although the earl said that he kept his lines as pure as possible, it's likely that at some point the dogs were bred with the retrievers that were being used in England before the fishermen arrived—to improve the local dogs. The Third Earl of Malmesbury gave some of his dogs to the Sixth Earl of Buccleigh, and it was he who actually started keeping good breeding records.

In 1904, the Kennel Club in Britain listed Labrador Retrievers as a separate breed. Before that time, *retriever* covered the broad category of all retrievers. Labs were gaining popularity by leaps and bounds, winning at field trials and in the ring at dog shows.

Labs started out as working dogs for fishermen. Their dense, waterproof coat and thick, paddlelike tail were assets.

The Lab in the USA

It's ironic that Labrador Retrievers, which were developed in North America, came to us from Britian. They were being exported to the United States and were popular before World War I. Although the AKC grouped them together with the other retrievers, those who were active in sport shooting considered the Labrador Retriever the best breed for waterfowlers. Many serious breeders from Long Island imported the dogs, as did expert kennel men and gamekeepers from Europe.

By the later part of the 1920s, the AKC recognized the Labrador Retriever as a separate breed. The Labrador Club of America was founded on Long Island late in 1930, and Mrs. Marshall Field became the first president, serving from 1931 to 1935. Franklin B. Lord and Robert Goelet were co-vice presidents. Mrs. Marshall Field judged the first specialty show in 1933. (A specialty show is

In the United States, Labs became the breed of choice for hunting waterfowl. Labs bred for field work tend to be more slender and taller.

What Is the AKC?

The American Kennel Club (AKC) is the oldest and largest pure-bred dog registry in the United States. Its main function is to record the pedigrees of dogs of the breeds it recognizes. While AKC registration papers are a guarantee that a dog is pure-bred, they are absolutely not a guarantee of the quality of the dog—as the AKC itself will tell you.

The AKC makes the rules for all the canine sporting events it sanctions and approves judges for those events. It is also involved in various public education programs and legislative efforts regarding dog ownership. More recently, the AKC has helped establish a foundation to study canine health issues and a program to register microchip numbers for companion animal owners. The AKC has no individual members—its members are national and local breed clubs and clubs dedicated to various competitive sports.

for only one breed.) It was held in a garage in New York City. Thirty-four dogs were entered, and the winner was Boli of Blake, owned by Lord.

In the 1920s and 1930s, when most Labrador Retrievers were being run in retrieving trials as well as competing in dog shows, many famous Long Island families were involved in these competitions. Some of them included the Phipps, the Marshall Fields, J. P. Morgan, Wilton Lloyd Smith, and the Whitneys.

The Lab Today

The Lab has soared in popularity in the United States, and has reigned as the most popular dog in the country (measured by AKC registrations) for more than a decade. Today's Labrador Retriever breeders are trying to develop dual-, triple-, and multipurpose Labs in an effort to demonstrate and maintain the breed's working instincts. Club members and breeders are encouraged to strive to breed Labrador Retrievers who look like Labs, hunt like Labs, and can perform a variety of jobs.

Labs bred for the show ring tend to be heavier and thicker.

Unfortunately, the breed's popularity has also created a big market for Labs, and this has resulted in many people breeding the dog for profit, either in puppy mills (commercial dog farms) or in family backyards. These people, even those who genuinely care about the breed, often know little about the breed standard, genetics, or the breed's health concerns, and so may turn out inferior dogs.

All of these variables have created several different types of Labrador Retrievers. Although these dogs may have some differences, they are still Labs, and each has a core of fanciers who love them. These are some of the different types seen.

- English Labrador Retrievers tend to be heavier boned, with a more pronounced, blocky head and a thicker body than the American Labs.
- American Labrador Retrievers, bred to show in conformation dog shows, are often from English lines, but many tend to be longer-legged, making them a little taller than their English relations.
- Labs bred to work in the field and compete in field trials are generally taller, more slender, and more athletic than their show dog cousins. The field Labs are also more active and have a very strong instinct to retrieve.
- Pet Labs vary according to their ancestry. Unfortunately, many pet Labs are small and lighter boned than they should be, and many do not have the trademark level, stable temperament of the Labrador Retriever.

People looking for a new Lab need to understand what their needs are as far as a dog is concerned and what their goals are for the dog. Obviously, if you would like to compete in conformation dog shows with your new dog, you will need a dog from show lines, purchased from a reputable breeder.

Chapter 3

Why Choose a Labrador Retriever?

Labrador Retriever puppies are round, fuzzy, clumsy little creatures with floppy feet sticking out at each corner. It's not hard to fall in love with this funny and affectionate puppy. However, Labs don't stay fuzzy puppies; they grow up to be big dogs weighing 60 to 80 pounds, and sometimes even more. The Lab can be a wonderful sporting dog and a devoted family companion, but he is not for everyone. He needs an owner who can provide him with leadership as well as companionship. He needs someone who can spend time with him and who enjoys training and dog sports. The Lab is a true companion dog. This is not a dog to leave alone in the backyard for hours each day.

Are You Ready for a Dog?

Adding a dog to your household should be a well-thought-out decision. You will be taking on the responsibility of a living, thinking, caring animal, who is willing to give his life for you. That's a big responsibility.

A dog should never be acquired on impulse. It's always best to think through what's involved in owning a dog and to be honest with yourself. So let's take a look at dog ownership and see if you can do what's needed for any dog, and then we'll look specifically at Labs.

Are you sure your other pets will enjoy having a dog?

- Do you have time for a dog? Dogs need your time for companionship, affection, play, and training. You cannot dash in the door, toss down some dog food, and leave again. That's not fair, and the dog will react badly to it.
- Do you live in a place where dogs are allowed and are welcome? If you rent your home, do you have permission from your landlord to have a dog? Not all neighborhoods and buildings are dog-friendly, so make sure a dog will be welcome before you bring one home.
- Who, besides yourself, is living with the dog? Is everyone in agreement about getting a dog? If you want the dog but someone else in the household is afraid or doesn't like the dog, that could become very difficult.
- Is there someone in the family who could have a hard time with the dog? Is there a baby in the house, someone who is very frail, or a senior citizen with poor balance? Dogs can be unaware of their strength and size, especially when they're puppies.
- Do you have other pets in the household? Will your cat enjoy having a dog in the house? You may have to protect your rabbit, ferret, or gerbil from a rambunctious puppy.
- Have you lived with a dog before? Do you know what to expect? Really? Dogs can shed, drag in dirt and leaves from outside, catch and kill a rodent and then throw up the remains on the living room sofa.

- Do you have the money to care for a dog? Dogs need to be spayed or neutered, need vaccinations, and may hurt themselves, requiring emergency veterinary care. Plus, you will need a dog crate, leash and collar, toys, and dog food.

Dog ownership is wonderful. Dogs are the ultimate confidants and never reveal your secrets. They are security in a scary world and the best friend a person could have. But only if you are really ready for the responsibilities of caring for one.

The Lab as a Pet

The Lab was originally bred to be a versatile dog, and was developed from hardworking dogs who performed many jobs, including retrieving both birds and fish. Most Labs, to varying degrees and depending upon their individual bloodlines, retain some of these working instincts. This has a definite effect on the dog's ability to be happy as a family companion and pet.

A dog from American show lines is usually a good choice as a pet, while field dogs may be too intense and driven to relax as a family pet. However, if a family member wants to participate in dog sports that require an intense, energetic dog—such as agility, flyball, dock diving, or search and rescue work—or if you plan to hunt with your dog, then a dog from field lines might be just right. Let's take a look at the breed as a whole, though, because all Labrador Retrievers have many traits in common.

Labs Are Not Small

The Labrador Retriever is considered a medium to large dog, averaging from 60 to 80 pounds when fully grown—although many are bigger. That means a 60- to 100-pound dog stretched out across the living room floor or curled up on the sofa. A dog this large does not go unnoticed in a household, and many times adjustments must be made.

Labs were born to retrieve, and all Labs have this working instinct.

With this size comes strength. The Lab is a powerful dog and without training could easily jump on and knock down a child, a senior citizen, or even an unprepared adult. Older puppies and young adults are unaware of their size and strength and can easily hurt people even though they have no intention of doing so. However, with training, the dog can learn to restrain that power.

Labs Are High-Energy Dogs

The Lab is a fairly high-energy dog who requires daily exercise—daily *strenuous* exercise. A two- or three-mile walk around the neighborhood would be good exercise for an older dog or a puppy, but cannot be considered adequate exercise for a healthy adult dog. A good run, a fast session of throwing the ball, or a jog alongside a bicycle is more appropriate.

Many Labs will bark, especially when they're playing, and it's important to make sure your neighbors won't be bothered by this. Lab puppies and adolescents are known to chew destructively on just about anything, from toys to your furniture, so you will need to be able to spend time training the puppy and making sure you can prevent bad behavior. Labs also love food, any food, and have been

Labs are high-energy dogs and will need a lot of exercise.

The Dog's Senses

The dog's eyes are designed so that he can see well in relative darkness, has excellent peripheral vision, and is very good at tracking moving objects—all skills that are important to a carnivore. Dogs also have good depth perception. Those advantages come at a price, though: Dogs are nearsighted and are slow to change the focus of their vision. It's a myth that dogs are colorblind. However, while they can see some (but not all) colors, their eyes were designed to most clearly perceive subtle shades of gray—an advantage when they are hunting in low light.

Dogs have about six times fewer taste buds on their tongue than humans do. They can taste sweet, sour, bitter, and salty tastes, but with so few taste buds, it's likely that their sense of taste is not very refined.

A dog's ears can swivel independently, like radar dishes, to pick up sounds and pinpoint their location. Dogs can locate a sound in $6/100$ of a second and hear sound four times farther away than we can (which is why there is no reason to yell at your dog). They can also hear sounds at far higher pitches than we can.

In their first few days of life, puppies primarily use their sense of touch to navigate their world. Whiskers on the face, above the eyes, and below the jaws are sensitive enough to detect changes in airflow. Dogs also have touch-sensitive nerve endings all over their bodies, including on their paws.

Smell may be a dog's most remarkable sense. Dogs have about 220 million scent receptors in their nose, compared to about 5 million in humans, and a large part of the canine brain is devoted to interpreting scent. Not only can dogs smell scents that are very faint, but they can also accurately distinguish between those scents. In other words, when you smell a pot of spaghetti sauce cooking, your dog probably smells tomatoes and onions and garlic and oregano and whatever else is in the pot.

> **Characteristics of a Lab**
>
> Strong retrieving instinct
>
> Acute senses of hearing and smell
>
> Loves to swim
>
> Keys to movement of birds
>
> Requires daily strenuous exercise
>
> Puppies can be destructive
>
> Sheds, especially in spring and fall
>
> Slow to mature

known to raid trash cans for tidbits. They will also, when they get a chance, steal food from the kitchen counter; so again, training and prevention are important. When bored, Labs will also try to escape from the yard when they don't get enough exercise. They don't do this maliciously; they're just looking for something to do. However, you'll find that when your Labrador Retriever has been exercised daily and practices his training skills, he will be healthier, happier, and more relaxed, and destructiveness around the house and yard will be minimal.

Labs Need a Job

Because the breed was developed from dogs who assisted their owners in many ways, Labs today need an occupation, something to keep the mind challenged and the body busy. There are quite a few different jobs you can give your Lab. Use the dog's obedience training to give him some structure in his life and to teach him to work for you and listen to your commands. Teach him to bring you your newspaper and find your slippers or keys. Teach him to find your kids by name. Find a dog training club in your area and try something new, like agility, scent hurdle races, or dock diving. Teach your dog to play Frisbee. All of these things will keep your Lab busy, focused, and happy.

Do You Have a Problem with Hair?

Labs shed. There is no way to get around it. Yes, that hair looks short, but the undercoat is thicker than you might think, and those short hairs stick in everything. Although the breed doesn't shed as much as many other breeds—Collies and German Shepherds, for example—that wonderful, weather-resistant coat does shed. If dog hair in the house bothers you, don't get a Lab. Living with a Lab requires a few compromises, and understanding that the dog sheds is one of them.

The worst shedding times are spring and fall, depending upon the climate, but some shedding takes place all year round. The easiest way to keep it under control is to brush the dog thoroughly every day.

Labs make fabulous family dogs, as long as you make sure to incorporate them into your family's daily activities.

Labs Are Slow to Mature

By the age of 2 years, many dogs are grown up—mentally and physically. Labs, however, are puppies for a long time. Physically, most Labs do not reach maturity until 3 or 4 years old. They are still filling out, getting that Lab chest, and their coat is maturing.

The aspect of this that bothers most pet owners is the breed's slow mental maturity. Labs are puppies a long time, and often are not mentally mature until 3 or 4 years of age. That means while some breeds can be trusted in the house not to get into trouble by 2 years of age, Labs may need to be 4. A 3-year-old Lab may still want to raid the trash can or get into the cat food. This is not a problem if you are aware of it. But many unsuspecting pet owners, especially those who have previously had puppies of other breeds, may assume that Labs grow up at the same rate and may be disappointed when their Lab doesn't.

The Working and Field Lab

Keeping a Lab as a family pet and companion means you need to be able to provide him with an outlet for the working and sporting instincts he was bred to have. You can teach him jobs to do at home, but you can also continue with your training and do much more with him.

- Therapy dogs are privately owned pets who, with their owner, visit nursing homes, day centers, schools, and other places to provide love and affection to people who need it. Labs make wonderful therapy dogs as soon as they have had some obedience training and are mature enough to control themselves, so they do not jump up on people.
- Agility is a dog sport that consists of the dog's leaping, jumping, running, and crawling through a number of different obstacles as his owner directs him where to go next. Most Labs are quite good at this sport.
- Flyball is a team relay sport. The dogs jump a series of small hurdles, press a lever in a box that shoots out a tennis ball, and then return back over the hurdles. Since Labs love tennis balls and are quite athletic, this sport is made to order for them.
- Dock diving is a new sport that Labs absolutely love! The dog runs hard and then jumps off an elevated platform into the water in pursuit of a toy. The dog who can jump the longest distance wins.
- Teaching your dog to pull a wagon requires maturity on the dog's part and training on yours, but it can be great fun and very useful.
- Obedience competition requires a great deal of training, but for those with a competitive streak, it's also great fun. Many Labs have done extremely well in this sport.
- The Labrador Retriever has a very good nose and tracking comes easily to him. Tracking can be for fun (just for training purposes), for competition, or for search and rescue work.
- Labs are also good hunting companions and are still the breed of choice for retrieving waterfowl.
- Search and rescue dogs are always needed. This volunteer activity is very time-consuming, however, and requires training for both the dog and the owner. It is very rewarding, and Labs are awesome at it.

If Labs Could Choose Their Owners

If a Labrador Retriever could choose his owner, rather than the other way around, he would probably choose an owner who likes to do stuff. Being active himself, the Lab would enjoy a companion who will go for walks, hike in the hills, throw the ball, go swimming, and train with firmness yet fun.

Labs also need an owner who will be a leader. A good leader is kind and caring yet firm. The leader provides the dog with guidance and security. Without a

Your Lab prefers an owner who is firm but fair, will keep him busy, and will make him an important part of your life.

strong leader, the Lab will remain silly and undisciplined, as well as physically strong and rowdy.

Labs also need an owner who is willing and able to train the dog, beginning in early puppyhood and continuing well into adulthood. Not only does this help establish leadership, but it also teaches this soon-to-be-large dog self-control. Training also occupies the dog's mind—something every Lab needs.

The owner of a Lab is in for a dog's lifetime of busyness. Lab puppies are silly, clumsy, and on the go all the time. But even when they are mentally and physically mature, Labs are still looking for something to do. The Lab will drop a tennis ball in your lap for you to throw or will bring you his leash—a hint that it's time for a walk. Gray-muzzled old Labs may enjoy time to snooze on the sofa, but even the old dogs still want to be a part of life and involved with everything that's going on. So the best owner for a Lab is someone who wants a real canine companion; someone who wants to share their life with a devoted dog.

Chapter 4

Choosing Your Labrador Retriever

Labrador Retrievers were bred to work for and with people. Unlike some other breeds (many terriers and the sighthounds, for example), Labs were not made to work alone. They are happiest when they spend the day side by side with their working partner. For the same reason, your new Lab will be happiest when she's by your side, able to share your activities and ready to do things for you. It's important, then, to make sure you choose your new companion wisely. Although any dog might be able to fit into your life, when you make an educated, well-researched choice your chances are much better of that dog being "the perfect one."

Breeder, Rescue, Shelter, or Free?

You can find a Labrador Retriever in many different places: from a breeder, from a Lab rescue group, at your local shelter, or even in a cardboard box outside the local grocery store. Although the puppy outside the grocery store will be the least expensive and you may feel good about saving the life of a dog at the local shelter, is one of those dogs really the right dog for you? Let's take a look at the pros and cons of each of these choices.

Reputable Breeders

A breeder is someone who breeds dogs of a specific breed, in this case Labrador Retrievers. A reputable breeder is someone who has been involved with the breed for a number of years and knows it well. They have studied the top dogs in the breed. In Labs, hopefully they have studied working and field dogs as well as show dogs. They know quite a bit about breed genetics, and they choose the sire (father) and dam (mother) of each litter carefully.

Reputable breeders show their dogs so that the judges (who are often also breeders) can evaluate the dogs. Some Lab breeders also compete in other sports, including agility, obedience, and field trials, or simply go out hunting with them.

These breeders should also be knowledgeable of the health prob-

Reputable breeders often compete in dog sports or simply hunt with their dogs. These activities prove the value of their breeding lines.

lems of the breed, especially because there are so many facing Labs today. As many health tests for inherited defects as are available should be performed before selecting the dogs to be used for breeding.

Reputable breeders will also screen the people who come to buy one of their dogs. The breeder will ask potential buyers to fill out an application and may ask for personal references. If you are not approved for one of their puppies, don't take it personally; the breeder is concerned about the welfare of their puppies, and they know their dogs best.

Backyard Breeders

A backyard breeder usually refers to someone who has bred their dog (usually a family pet) but who does not have the knowledge a reputable breeder has. Many times the dog(s) being bred are simply treasured family pets, and the owner breeds the dog(s) in the hopes of creating another dog just like their pet. Genetics doesn't work that way, though, and they end up with a litter of puppies for sale that may or may not be quality dogs.

Lab Rescue

Purebred rescue groups are organized by people who love their breed and are concerned about the dogs who need new homes—especially those who might otherwise be killed for want of a good home. Some groups are run by breed clubs, while others are private organizations.

You will be asked to fill out an application, and some groups even ask for a home visit. They want to know that your fence is high and strong enough to keep in a Lab and that you and your family understand the realities of owning this breed.

Labs in Local Shelters

A Labrador Retriever can end up in a local shelter for many reasons. Her owner may have passed away and no one in the family wanted her. Someone may have purchased a Lab puppy without researching the breed and after a few months realized the dog was too much for them. The dog may have escaped from the yard and was picked up as a stray and no one bailed her out. There are many reasons, and many of them are not the dog's fault at all.

A Lab in the shelter is basically an unknown. She may have been produced by a wonderful, reputable breeder, or she may have come from a commercial puppy farm. Although the dog's physical appearance can give you some clues, sometimes it's really hard to tell. The dog's temperament is also an unknown because a Lab in a shelter is going to be stressed and very unhappy; she is not going to show her real personality until she's in a home and settles down.

Really nice dogs can end up in shelters or rescue groups, and may be available for adoption.

Labs for Free

Have you heard the adage "You get what you pay for"? That Lab puppy in the box outside the grocery store is probably the result of backyard breeding, maybe even an accidental breeding. The dog could be a mix; the father may even be unknown. And although mixed-breed dogs can be great pets, you'll be disappointed if you were looking for a purebred Lab.

The puppy (and maybe even the mother dog) may or may not have had any veterinary care, which could mean no vaccinations, no worming, and no preventive health care. The person who owned the mother dog most likely never heard of socialization, so the puppy will not have had any planned socialization.

Choosing Your Lab

Service dog trainers, many of whom use Labs in their programs, have developed puppy tests that help them evaluate puppies' responses to specific stimuli, which helps them choose puppies for certain kinds of service dog work. The service dog trainers are then able to train only those dogs who have the temperament, character, and personality traits best suited for the specific work.

Puppy tests can help you, too, because you can use them to choose the best dog for you, your family, and your goals. The tests are best done when the puppy is 6 to 7 weeks old. Many breeders do puppy tests, and if your dog's breeder does, ask if you can watch. If the breeder normally doesn't test the puppies, ask if you can do it. They may be interested enough in the results to say yes.

To get started, list all the puppies on a sheet of paper. If several look alike, put different-colored ribbons or little collars on each of them.

Labrador Retriever clubs can be a good source for finding reputable breeders.

Look at the Whole Litter

Without getting involved (no petting right now), just watch the entire litter. By 6 weeks of age, the puppies will be playing with each other, bouncing around, tripping over each other and their own big paws. Make some notes about their behavior. The boldest puppy, who is often also the biggest, is usually the first to do anything. She is the first to the food, the first to check out a new toy, and the first to investigate anything new. This is a good working puppy. She would not be a good choice for someone who lives alone and works long hours, nor would she be a good dog for someone with a less than dominant personality.

Puppy Temperament Test

Have your paper at hand and make notes as you go along, or better yet, have someone else make notes for you. Test each puppy individually. Don't look at your notes until you're done.

Walk away. Place the puppy on the ground at your feet. Stand up and walk away. Does the puppy:

a. Follow you.
b. Put herself underfoot, climbing on your feet.
c. Do a belly crawl to follow you.
d. Ignore you and go the other direction.

Call the puppy. Move away from the puppy, then bend over and call her, spreading your hands and arms wide to encourage her. Does the puppy:

a. Come to you, tail wagging.
b. Chase you so fast that you don't have a chance to call her.
c. Come slowly or crawl on her belly to you.
d. Ignore you.

The fearful puppy will sit in the corner by herself, just watching what her brothers and sisters are doing. Her tail will be tight to her hindquarters, and she may duck her head. Unfortunately, fearful, neurotic Labs are not unknown. Although some fearful puppies come out of their shell with a calm, caring, knowledgeable owner, these dogs usually retain some of their fear all their lives. These dogs are not good for noisy, active households or for first-time dog owners. Even with a knowledgeable owner, these dogs can often be a problem.

Most puppies fall somewhere in between these two extremes. In one situation, the puppy may be bold and outgoing, and in another, she may fall back to watch. While you're watching, look to see who is the crybaby, who is the troublemaker, and who always gets the toy. Jot down notes.

Most puppies fall somewhere in between these two extremes. In one situation, a puppy may be bold and outgoing and in another, she may fall back to watch. While you're watching, look to see who is the crybaby, who is the troublemaker, and who always gets the toy. Jot down notes.

Now it's time for the test. You'll find it in the box above.

Gentle restraint. Pick up the puppy and gently roll her over so she's on her back in your arms. Place a hand on her chest to gently restrain her for thirty seconds—no longer. Does she:

- a. Struggle for a few seconds, then relax.
- b. Struggle for the entire thirty seconds.
- c. Cry, tuck her tail up, and perhaps urinate.
- d. Struggle for fifteen seconds, stop, then look at you or look away.

Lifting. When the puppy is on the ground, place both hands under her ribcage and lift her paws off the ground for thirty seconds. Does the puppy:

- a. Quietly accept it with just a little wiggling.
- b. Struggle for at least fifteen seconds.
- c. Accept it with a tucked tail.
- d. Struggle for more than fifteen seconds.

Toss a ball. With the puppy close to you, show her a ball and then toss it just a few feet away. Does the puppy:

- a. Dash after it, pick it up, and bring it back to you.
- b. Bring it back but doesn't want to give it back to you.
- c. Go after it but does not pick it up, or gets distracted.
- d. Pick it up but walks away.

Looking at the Results

There are no right or wrong answers. This is a guide to help you choose the right puppy for you—and even then, this is only a guide. Puppies can change as they grow up.

The puppy who scored mostly A's is a middle-of-the-pack dog in terms of dominance. This is neither the most dominant puppy nor the most submissive. If she also scored an A in the ball test, this puppy will suit most families with children or active couples. This puppy should accept training well, and although she may have some challenges during adolescence, she will grow up to be a nice dog.

The puppy who scored mostly A's and B's will be a little more dominant, a little more pushy. If she scored a B or a D on the ball test, you may find training to be somewhat of a challenge.

The puppy who scored mostly B's is a more dominant puppy. She could be a great working dog with the right owner. She needs an owner who has a more

Begin by looking at the whole litter without interacting with the puppies. That's not easy!

forceful personality; she is not the right dog for a passive person. She will need structured training from puppyhood on into adulthood.

The puppy who scored mostly C's will need special handling, as this puppy is very worried about life. She could, if pushed too far, bite out of fear. She needs a calm environment and a calm, confident owner.

The puppy who scored C's and D's may have trouble bonding with people. However, if she finds the right owner, she will bond and will be very devoted. This puppy needs calm, careful, patient training.

The puppy who scored mostly D's doesn't think she needs people. She is very self-confident and will need to spend a lot of time with her owner so she can develop a relationship. If she spends too much time alone, she may not bond with a person at all.

Now What?

After looking at the puppies, testing them all, figuring out the results, and perhaps narrowing the litter down to two or three puppies, what's next? Which puppy appeals to you the most? Which puppy keeps returning to you? Which one makes your heart go thump-thump?

Although these tests can help narrow your choices, you still need to listen to your heart. So think logically and then let your heart work with your brain to choose the right puppy for you.

Choosing an Adult Lab

A puppy is all potential. She is the result of her genetics and the care she's received as a baby, but other than that, she's just ready for the world. An adult, on the other hand, is already formed. What you see is what you're going to get. If you want a big Lab or a smaller one, or if you want a bold dog or a quieter one, the adult dog is already what she is going to be.

The adult dog also has a history. Perhaps she was in a loving home and lost that home due to a divorce or a death in the family. She may have been in a home where she was neglected or even mistreated. The things that happened to her have shaped who she is—she may always be worried about large men with sticks in their hands, or she may always be attracted to older women.

Although some Labs can hold a grudge for a long time, they are, for the most part, very forgiving. Many Labs who have lost a home, good or bad, will grieve for that home when they lose it. Labs are very devoted and will love even the worst owner. When allowed to grieve, they will, but then they will accept and adapt to a new home.

Tests used on baby puppies do not work on adult dogs; so when adopting an adult dog, you need to rely on any information you can get from the people who have been caring for her.

It is important, though, to find out as much as you can about the dog and her first home so that you can help her adjust to your home. If the shelter people say she appears afraid of brooms, for example, once she's in your home, ask a trainer or behaviorist for help desensitizing her to brooms.

Many adult Labs are looking for good homes.

Part II

Caring for Your Labrador Retriever

Chapter 5

Getting Ready for Your Labrador Retriever

Bringing home your new dog (or puppy) is a wonderful time. But before you give in to all this excitement, you need to prepare for your new friend. Let's make sure your yard and house are ready, and that you have everything you'll need. If you're prepared, you won't have to worry about anything and can spend the time at home with your new dog.

Basic Supplies

The box on page 43 outlines most of the basics you will need for your dog. We discuss dog foods in more detail in chapter 6, but for now, just plan on having a supply on hand of the food the dog has been eating. If you decide to change foods, you'll want to do that very gradually so that your new dog doesn't end up with a tummy ache.

You will want to put some identification on your new Lab right away. Most pet stores sell identification tags, both the engraved ones and the temporary ones. Just make sure your phone numbers (home and cell) are on the dog's tag. You can get one with his name later, once you've figured out what to name him. Put the tag on a buckle collar (nylon or leather) that will be on him all the time. If you're bringing home a puppy, you'll have to replace that collar a couple of times as he grows.

Puppy Essentials

You'll need to go shopping *before* you bring your puppy home. There are many, many adorable and tempting items at pet supply stores, but these are the basics.

- **Food and water dishes.** Look for bowls that are wide and low or weighted in the bottom so they will be harder to tip over. Stainless steel bowls are a good choice because they are easy to clean (plastic never gets completely clean) and almost impossible to break. Avoid bowls that place the food and water side by side in one unit—it's too easy for your dog to get his water dirty that way.
- **Leash.** A six-foot leather leash will be easy on your hands and very strong.
- **Collar.** Start with a nylon buckle collar. For a perfect fit, you should be able to insert two fingers between the collar and your pup's neck. Your dog will need larger collars as he grows up.
- **Crate.** Choose a sturdy crate that is easy to clean and large enough for your puppy to stand up, turn around, and lie down in. You will need either a large crate that can be sectioned off for while your puppy is small or you'll need to get a couple of different crates as he grows up.
- **Nail cutters.** Get a good, sharp pair that are the appropriate size for the nails you will be cutting. A large pair of scissors-type clippers work well for German Shepherds, but your dog's breeder or veterinarian can also give you some guidance here.
- **Grooming tools.** Different kinds of dogs need different kinds of grooming tools. See chapter 7 for advice on what to buy.
- **Chew toys.** Dogs *must* chew, especially puppies. Make sure you get things that won't break or crumble off in little bits, which the dog can choke on. Very hard rubber bones are a good choice. Dogs love rawhide bones, too, but pieces of the rawhide can get caught in your dog's throat, so they should be allowed only when you are there to supervise. Chew toys must be large enough that the dog cannot inadvertently swallow them.
- **Toys.** Watch for sharp edges and unsafe items such as plastic eyes that can be swallowed. Many toys come with squeakers, which dogs can also tear out and swallow. The toys, including balls, should be large enough so the dog cannot choke on them. All dogs will eventually destroy their toys; as each toy is torn apart, replace it with a new one.

A leash is also a necessity so you can restrain your new dog as you bring him home, take him to the veterinarian, and for your walks together. Don't ever take your Lab outside of your house or yard off-leash; not only is it illegal in most places, but your dog could also dash away from you and get hit by a car, or get lost.

Make Your Yard Safe

Labrador Retrievers are companion dogs and prefer to spend all of their time with you. However, they do need to be outside sometimes to get some sunshine and exercise and to relieve themselves. It's also important that you allow your Lab some time away from you now and then, too, even if he's not happy about it, so that he doesn't get worried when you go to work, or the store, or to visit friends. Let him spend an hour or two each day outside in your yard as long as the yard is safe and secure.

A six-foot-high, solid (so the dog cannot see through it) fence is best for a Lab. It can be a solid wooden fence or a concrete block wall. A chain link fence the dog can see through is not a good idea, because your Lab may decide to bark at everything he sees. This can lead to problem barking.

If your fence is not secure or if you would like to protect some parts of your yard, you can build a dog run. It should be large enough to provide your dog with room to move around and room to relieve himself away from his favorite place to bask in the sun. Since Labs can be diggers, the floor of the run should be concrete or should have wire fencing under the dirt or sand substrate.

Your dog should always have some shade and shelter from the weather. This can be a shade awning, a large tree, or even access to the garage. Very few Labs will use a doghouse, so this will be wasted. (You will see your Lab outside, even in the rain, because most Labs love water and their waterproof coat protects them.)

He should also have a source of fresh, clean water. A five-gallon galvanized tub works well because it's large enough that the water can stay cool and heavy enough that the dog cannot dump it over.

There are some supplies every dog needs, and lots of other things that are just fun to buy.

Your dog can spend a little time alone in the yard, if it is safe and secure. But Labs will not do well spending long stretches confined to the yard without their family.

When Your Dog First Comes Home

You're going to be excited when you first bring home your new Labrador Retriever, and chances are, you're going to want to share that excitement. Restrain yourself right now for your new dog's sake. Although Labs are very social dogs, your new best friend needs to get to know you and bond with you before he meets other people.

Bonding is the process of developing a relationship. When he is bonded with you, he will care about you and will want to be with you. When you are bonded with him, you will do anything to keep him safe. This bonding takes a little time— at least a weekend—so be selfish and keep him at home with you and your family.

Later it will be important for him to meet your neighbors, friends, and extended family so he can become socialized to other people. Just keep the get-togethers brief and control the meetings. Don't let people get rough with the puppy, even in play, and let just one or two people meet him at a time. Never let a group of people gang up on him; even the most social Lab could be frightened by that.

Crate Training

Adding a Lab puppy or dog to your household can be a wonderful experience, but it can sour quickly if the dog is ruining your carpets and chewing up your

Puppy-Proofing Your Home

You can prevent much of the destruction puppies can cause and keep your new dog safe by looking at your home and yard from a dog's point of view. Get down on all fours and look around. Do you see loose electrical wires, cords dangling from the blinds, or chewy shoes on the floor? Your pup will see them too!

In the kitchen:
- Put all knives and other utensils away in drawers.
- Get a trash can with a tight-fitting lid.
- Put all household cleaners in cupboards that close securely; consider using childproof latches on the cabinet doors.

In the bathroom:
- Keep all household cleaners, medicines, vitamins, shampoos, bath products, perfumes, makeup, nail polish remover, and other personal products in cupboards that close securely; consider using childproof latches on the cabinet doors.
- Get a trash can with a tight-fitting lid.
- Don't use toilet bowl cleaners that release chemicals into the bowl every time you flush.
- Keep the toilet bowl lid down.
- Throw away potpourri and any solid air fresheners.

In the bedroom:
- Securely put away all potentially dangerous items, including medicines and medicine containers, vitamins and supplements, perfumes, and makeup.
- Put all your jewelry, barrettes, and hairpins in secure boxes.
- Pick up all socks, shoes, and other chewables.

In the rest of the house:
- Tape up or cover electrical cords; consider childproof covers for unused outlets.
- Knot or tie up any dangling cords from curtains, blinds, and the telephone.

- Securely put away all potentially dangerous items, including medicines and medicine containers, vitamins and supplements, cigarettes, cigars, pipes and pipe tobacco, pens, pencils, felt-tip markers, craft and sewing supplies, and laundry products.
- Put all houseplants out of reach.
- Move breakable items off low tables and shelves.
- Pick up all chewable items, including television and electronics remote controls, cell phones, shoes, socks, slippers and sandals, food, dishes, cups and utensils, toys, books and magazines, and anything else that can be chewed on.

In the garage:

- Store all gardening supplies and pool chemicals out of reach of the dog.
- Store all antifreeze, oil, and other car fluids securely, and clean up any spills by hosing them down for at least ten minutes.
- Put all dangerous substances on high shelves or in cupboards that close securely; consider using childproof latches on the cabinet doors.
- Pick up and put away all tools.
- Sweep the floor for nails and other small, sharp items.

In the yard:

- Put the gardening tools away after each use.
- Make sure the kids put away their toys when they're finished playing.
- Keep the pool covered or otherwise restrict your pup's access to it when you're not there to supervise.
- Secure the cords on backyard lights and other appliances.
- Inspect your fence thoroughly. If there are any gaps or holes in the fence, fix them.
- Make sure you have no toxic plants in the garden.

A crate takes advantage of a pup's instinct to keep his den clean.

shoes. Two types of crates are commonly used. The first is a heavy plastic molded carrier, much like those the airlines require. The second is made of heavy metal wire bars. That's why you need a crate. Whichever you choose, it should be large enough for an adult dog to stand up, turn around, and lie down.

Introduce the crate to your puppy by opening the door and tossing a treat or toy inside. Allow the puppy to come and go as he pleases and to investigate the crate. When he is going in and out after a few treats, give him a treat and close the door. Leave the door closed for a few minutes and then let the puppy out if, and only if, he is being quiet. If the puppy is throwing a temper tantrum, don't let him out. If you do, you will have taught your puppy that a temper tantrum works to get him what he wants.

Put the puppy in his crate when you are home and can't supervise him, or when you are busy, such as eating a meal. Put the puppy in the crate when he is overstimulated—time-outs are good for puppies, too. And, of course, put the puppy in his crate for the night.

Never leave the puppy in the crate longer than four hours, except at night when the crate is next to your bed. It takes a while for the puppy to develop good bowel and bladder control, and you need to be able to let the puppy out when it's time.

Prevention

Many of the commonly seen problems with dogs can be avoided through simple prevention. Puppy-proofing your house is one means of prevention. Supervising the dog is another. Your Labrador Retriever can't chew up your sofa if you supervise him while he's in the house with you and you put him in his crate or outside in his pen when you can't watch him. By supervising the dog, you can teach him what is allowed and what is not. Using the sofa as an example again, if your Lab puppy decides to take a nibble out of the sofa cushion and you are paying attention, you can tell the puppy, "Aack! No!" as he grabs the cushion. Then you follow through by handing your puppy one of his chew toys: "Here, chew this instead."

The same can occur with food. Labs love food, and even when well fed, they will try to steal any food they can find. By practicing prevention—putting away food, keeping things picked up, and putting the cat's food out of the dog's reach—you can stop bad behavior before it happens.

Give your puppy appropriate chew toys and make sure you don't leave inappropriate things lying around for him to grab and destroy.

The thing your dog wants and needs most for all his life is to spend time with you.

Time with Your Dog

As I have mentioned several times, Labrador Retrievers are very people-oriented and must spend time with their owners. Your dog should be inside with you when you are home and next to your bed at night, except for his trips outside to relieve himself. In addition, you will need to make time to play with your dog, train him, and make sure he gets enough exercise.

With a little thought, it's amazing how creative people can be with their schedules. To spend time with your dog in the morning, getting up thirty minutes earlier will give you time for a fifteen- to twenty-minute walk before taking your shower. If you work close to home, your lunch hour might be just enough time to get home and eat your lunch as you throw the Frisbee for your dog. In the evening, take the children with you as you walk the dog; you can find out what's going on with the kids as you exercise and train your dog.

Pet Professionals

Although dogs have been our companions for thousands of years, you will find that you need some help with your new dog. Enlisting the help of some experienced pet professionals can help you keep your dog healthy, well behaved, and well cared for throughout his lifetime.

Veterinarian

The veterinarian to whom you choose to give your business will become your partner in your dog's continued good health. Like a family physician, the veterinarian will get to know your dog, will keep records on his weight and physical condition, and will help you get your dog through any health challenges.

When choosing a vet, call and make an appointment and go in without your dog. Expect to pay for an office call, since you are taking up the vet's time. Then ask some questions. The first one should be "Do you like Labrador Retrievers?" If your vet has had some bad experiences with the breed, they may prefer not to work with them. You don't want someone taking care of your dog who dislikes the breed or who is afraid of them.

If the veterinarian likes the breed, ask about their veterinary experience, office practices, and policies. What problems do they normally see with the breed and how do they handle those issues? How do they handle emergencies or after-hours problems?

When you have had a thorough discussion with the vet, and it seems the two of you will be able to work together, make another appointment for your dog. You want to make sure your new dog is healthy and to get him started on vaccinations or other health care needs.

Trainer

Just as with the veterinarian, find a trainer who likes Labs. Ask about their experience with the breed, what problems they have seen and how they handle them. If you see a well-behaved, nicely trained Lab when you are out for a walk, ask where the owner took their dog for training.

Every trainer has their own training technique, so go and watch one of this trainer's classes or training sessions. Make sure you will be happy with their training style and technique before you sign up for classes.

Chapter 6

Feeding Your
Labrador Retriever

A healthy Labrador Retriever has bright, alert eyes, and a shiny coat, and conveys the impression of power and unlimited energy. Although good health comes from many things, including the dog's genetic heritage and her overall care and environment, good nutrition is vitally important to good health. Many dogs can live well on a substandard diet. Unfortunately for those dogs, though, the lack of good nutrition will eventually catch up with them. Malnourishment usually shows up first as skin problems (itching, flaking, or redness), coat problems (dry coat, lack of shine, or a thinning coat), and immune system problems (the dog is often sick).

As with all dogs, the Labrador Retriever's body requires certain substances, and without them she could develop behavior problems, immune system deficiencies, susceptibility to disease, and, eventually, a much shorter life span. The pet food recalls of 2007 taught us that we can no longer take dog and cat foods for granted. We, as pet owners, must be advocates for our own pets' good health, including their nutrition. We must be educated, we must read labels, and we cannot be afraid to ask questions. In addition, we should take all advertising with the proverbial grain of salt!

Feeding Your Dog

Some dog owners like to fill a bowl of dog food and leave it out all day, letting the dog munch at will. Although it may be convenient, it is not a good idea for several reasons. First of all, the bowl of food may attract pests—even indoors. In addition, the food could become rancid.

When you are housetraining your puppy, free feeding makes it difficult to set up a routine. Your puppy will need to relieve herself after eating, and if she munches all day long, you won't be able to tell when she should go outside.

Last, but certainly not least, your dog needs to know that you are the giver of the food, and how better for her to learn it than when you hand her a bowl twice a day? If the food is always available, you are not the one giving it; it's always there—at least as far as your dog is concerned.

How Much?

Each and every Labrador Retriever needs a different amount of food. The dog's individual body metabolism, activity rate, and lifestyle all affect her nutritional needs.

Most dog food manufacturers print a chart on the bag showing how much to feed your dog. It's important to note that these are *suggested* guidelines. Labs are very efficient when digesting their food and tend to gain weight very easily. The amount of food listed on a bag of commercial food is often way too much for a Lab; the dog who eats that much will gain weight. Because Labs do tend to gain weight and obesity is a potential problem, watch your dog closely and measure

Most experts recommend feeding puppies two or three times a day. Pups need a lot of energy to grow, but little tummies can hold only so much food.

Labs tend to gain weight, so be sure to give your dog healthy snacks, and watch how much you feed her.

her food. Don't just fill a bowl and put it down; instead, measure the food by cups or scoops, and if the dog gains weight, cut back the amount you're feeding.

A healthy, well-nourished dog will have bright eyes, an alert expression, a shiny coat, supple skin, and energy to work and play. Although the Lab has a stocky body, even they should have a waistline that is visible from the side and from above. She should have meat and muscle on the bones, but you should still be able to feel the dog's ribs through the muscle. If the Lab has no waistline, you can't feel her ribs, and the dog is moving slowly and runs out of energy, it's time to see your veterinarian and find out if your dog is too heavy.

Mealtimes

Most experts recommend that puppies eat two to three times a day and adult dogs eat once or twice a day. Most dogs do very well with two meals, ten or twelve hours apart; so feed your dog after you eat breakfast and then again after you have dinner.

While you are eating, don't feed your Lab from the table or toss her scraps. This will cause her to beg from anyone at the table—a very bad habit. Don't toss her leftovers as you are cooking, either. That can lead to begging and even stealing in the kitchen. Don't forget that your Lab will be tall enough to reach the kitchen counter when she's grown up!

Snacks

An occasional dog biscuit or some training treats will not spoil your Lab's appetite, but don't get in the habit of offering treats just for the pleasure of it. Many American dogs are overweight, and obesity is a leading killer of dogs. When you do offer treats, offer either treats made specifically for dogs or something that is low in calories and nutritious, like a carrot. Don't offer candy, cookies, leftover tacos, or anything like that. Your Labrador Retriever doesn't need sugar, chocolate is deadly for dogs, and spicy foods can cause diarrhea and an upset stomach. Play it safe and give your Lab good-quality, nutritious snacks—very sparingly.

Pet Food vs. People Food

Many of the foods we eat are excellent sources of nutrients—after all, we do just fine on them. But dogs, just like us, need the right combination of meat and other ingredients for a complete and balanced diet, and simply giving the dog a bowl of meat doesn't provide that. In the wild, dogs eat the fur, skin, bones, and guts of their prey, and sometimes even the contents of the stomach.

This doesn't mean your dog can't eat what you eat. If your dog is eating a commercial dog food, you can still give her a little meat, dairy, bread, some fruits, or vegetables as a treat. Fresh foods have natural enzymes that processed foods don't have. Just remember, we're talking about the same food you eat, not the gristly, greasy leftovers you would normally toss in the trash. Stay away from sugar, too, and remember that chocolate is toxic to dogs.

If you want to share your food with your dog, be sure the total amount you give her each day doesn't make up more than 15 percent of her diet, and that the rest of what you feed her is a top-quality complete and balanced dog food. (More people food could upset the balance of nutrients in the commercial food.)

Can your dog eat an entirely homemade diet? Certainly, if you are willing to work at it. Any homemade diet will have to be carefully balanced, with all the right nutrients in just the right amounts. It requires a lot of research to make a proper homemade diet, but it can be done. It's best to work with a veterinary nutritionist.

If your dog is in training and you are using training treats, use good ones—nutritious treats—and cut back on all other treats. Training treats can be tiny pieces of cooked meats such as chicken or beef; just dice the pieces very small and put them in a sandwich bag. You can even freeze them before use. These make much better training treats than high-calorie commercial treats.

Nutritional Building Blocks

Nutrition is a constantly ongoing process that starts at conception and ends only with death. Everything that is consumed becomes part of the dog's daily nutrition, whether it's good for her or not. What the dog eats, the food's actual digestibility, and how the dog's body uses that food can all affect the actual nutrition gained by eating.

Although a dog can eat many things, including a lot of materials that may not be good for her, there are some substances she must eat regularly to keep her healthy. These can be a part of the commercial dog food you feed her, part of a homemade diet, or in the supplements added to her food.

Protein

Proteins are a varied group of biological compounds that affect many different functions in your Labrador Retriever's body, including the immune system, cell structure, and growth. As omnivores (dogs eat meat as well as some plant materials), dogs can digest protein from several sources. The most common are meats, grains, dairy products, and legumes. Recommendations vary as to how much of the dog's diet should be protein, but in general, most nutritionists agree that a diet that contains between 20 to 40 percent quality protein is good for a dog.

Carbohydrates

Carbohydrates, like proteins, have many functions in the dog's body, including serving as structural components of cells. However, the most important function is as an energy source. Carbohydrates can be obtained from many sources, including tubers (such as potatoes and sweet potatoes), plants (such as greens like broccoli and collard greens), and cereals. However, dogs do not have the necessary digestive enzymes to adequately digest all cereal grains. Therefore, the better sources of carbohydrates are tubers and noncitrus fruits, such as apples and bananas. Most experts recommend that a dog's diet contain from 20 to 40 percent carbohydrates of the right kind.

> **TIP**
>
> Don't forget to wash your dog's bowl after each meal. The leftover food particles and her saliva can cause a bacteria buildup in the bowl. Although she may not get sick right away, if the bacteria continue to build, she will. The water bowl should be cleaned regularly, too.

Reading Dog Food Labels

Dog food labels are not always easy to read, but if you know what to look for they can tell you a lot about what your dog is eating.

- The label should have a statement saying the dog food meets or exceeds the American Association of Feed Control Officials (AAFCO) nutritional guidelines. If the dog food doesn't meet AAFCO guidelines, it can't be considered complete and balanced, and can cause nutritional deficiencies.
- The guaranteed analysis lists the minimum percentages of crude protein and crude fat and the maximum percentages of crude fiber and water. AAFCO requires a minimum of 18 percent crude protein for adult dogs and 22 percent crude protein for puppies on a dry matter basis (that means with the water removed; canned foods have less protein because they have more water). Dog food must also have a minimum of 5 percent crude fat for adults and 8 percent crude fat for puppies.
- The ingredients list the most common item in the food first, and so on until you get to the least common item, which is listed last.
- Look for a dog food that lists an animal protein source first, such as chicken or poultry meat, and that has other protein sources listed among the top five ingredients. That's because a food that lists chicken, wheat, wheat gluten, corn, and wheat fiber as the first five ingredients has more chicken than wheat, but may not have more chicken than all the grain products put together.
- Other ingredients may include a digestible carbohydrate source (such as sweet potatoes or squash), fat, vitamins and minerals, preservatives, fiber, and sometimes other additives purported to be healthy.
- Some grocery store or generic brands may add artificial colors, sugar, and fillers—all of which should be avoided.

Fat

Fats have many uses in the body. They are the most important way the body stores energy. Fats also make up some of the structural elements of cells and are vital to the absorption of several vitamins. Certain fats are also beneficial in keeping the skin and coat healthy. Fats in dog foods are found primarily in meat and dairy products. Recommended levels are from 10 to 20 percent.

Vitamins

Vitamins are vital elements necessary for growth and the maintenance of life. There are two classes of vitamins: water-soluble and fat-soluble. Water-soluble vitamins include the B-complex vitamins and vitamin C. Fat-soluble vitamins include A, D, E, and K.

Water-Soluble Vitamins

These are absorbed by the body during digestion using the water found in the dog's food. Although it's usually a good idea to allow the dog to drink water whenever she's thirsty, additional water is not needed for digestion of these vitamins, because the water in the dog's body is sufficient as long as the dog is not dehydrated. Excess water-soluble vitamins are excreted from the body in the urine; so it's difficult to oversupplement these vitamins—although too much vitamin C can cause diarrhea.

The B vitamins serve a number of functions, including the metabolism of carbohydrates and amino acids. The B vitamins are very involved in many biochemical processes, and deficiencies can show up as weight loss, slow growth, dry and flaky skin, or anemia, depending upon the specific deficiency. The B vitamins can be obtained from meat and dairy products, beans, and eggs.

Vitamin C is a powerful antioxidant and, at the same time, a controversial vitamin. Some respected sources state that it is not a required dietary supplement for dogs, yet others regard C as a miracle vitamin. Some feel it can help prevent hip dysplasia and other potential problems, but these claims have not been proven. Dogs can produce a certain amount of vitamin C in their bodies, but this amount is often not sufficient, especially if the dog is under stress from work, injury, or illness.

A dog can eat many things, including a lot of things that may not be good for her. Keep a watchful eye on what your dog scavenges.

Fat-Soluble Vitamins

These vitamins require some fats in the dog's diet for adequate absorption. Fats are in the meat in your dog's diet and are added to commercial dog foods. Excess fat-soluble vitamins are stored in the body's fat. Excess vitamins of this type can cause problems, including toxicity. These vitamins should be added to the diet with care.

Vitamin A deficiencies show up as slow or retarded growth, reproductive failure, and skin and vision problems. Green and yellow vegetables are excellent sources of vitamin A, as are carrots, fish oils, and animal livers. The vegetables should be lightly cooked so the dog can digest them.

Vitamin D is needed for the correct absorption of calcium and phosphorus, and is necessary for the growth and development of bones and teeth and for muscle strength. Many dogs will produce a certain

We need to be wise consumers when it comes to feeding our dogs and carefully scrutinize the dog foods we buy.

amount of vitamin D when exposed to sunlight; however, often that is not enough and supplementation is needed. Balanced dog foods will generally have vitamin D in sufficient quantities.

Vitamin E is a powerful antioxidant that also works with several enzymes in the body. It has been shown to be effective in maintaining heart health and the immune system. It is also vital to other bodily systems, including the blood, nerves, muscles, and skin.

Vitamin K is needed for the proper clotting of blood. It is also important for healthy bones. Vitamin K is produced in the intestinal tract and normally supplementation is not needed. However, if the dog is having digestion problems or is on antibiotics, supplementation may be required. Vitamin K can be found in dark green vegetables, including kale and spinach. These should be lightly cooked before feeding them to your dog.

Minerals

Minerals, like vitamins, are necessary for life and physical well-being. Minerals can affect the body in many ways. A deficiency of calcium can lead to rickets, a deficiency of manganese can cause reproductive failure, and a zinc deficiency can lead to growth retardation and skin problems.

Many minerals are tied in with vitamins; in other words, a vitamin deficiency will also result in a mineral deficiency. For example, an adequate amount of vitamin B_{12} ensures there is also an adequate amount of cobalt because cobalt, a mineral, is a constituent of B_{12}.

Water is as important a component of your dog's diet as all the other nutrients.

Minerals are normally added to commercial dog foods. If you're feeding a homemade diet, that can be supplemented with a vitamin and mineral tablet to make sure the dog has sufficient minerals.

Water

It may seem like common sense to say that your Labrador Retriever will need water, but the importance of water cannot be emphasized enough. Water makes up about 70 percent of a dog's weight. Water facilitates the generation of energy, the transportation of nutrients, and the disposal of wastes. Water is in the bloodstream, in the eyes, in the cerebrospinal fluid, and in the gastrointestinal tract. Water is vital to all of the body's functions in some way.

Commercial Dog Foods

Dog food sales in the United States are a huge business with tremendous competition among manufacturers. Dog owners should understand that, as a big business, these companies' goals include making a profit. Although advertising may show a dog and owner in a warm and fuzzy, heart-tugging moment, the nutrition your dog might get from the food being advertised has nothing to do with that heart-tugging moment. It's all about getting you to buy the food.

Dog owners must be wise consumers, and we cannot let the pet food recall of 2007 fade into memory. Read the dog food labels, check out the manufacturers' Web sites, check the recall lists, and talk to dog food experts, including your veterinarian if they have a background in nutrition.

A good-quality food is necessary for your Labrador Retriever's health. Dog foods vary in quality, from the very good to the terrible. To make sure you are using a high-quality food, read the labels on the packages (see the box on page 57). Make sure the food offers the levels of protein, carbohydrates, and fats recommended earlier in this chapter.

Read the list of ingredients, too. If one of the first ingredients listed is by-products, be leery of the food. By-products are the parts of slaughtered animals that are not muscle meat—lungs, spleen, kidneys, brain, liver, blood, bone, fatty tissue, stomach, and intestines. Dog food manufacturers can meet protein requirements by including by-products, but they are inferior forms of protein that do not metabolize as completely in the dog's body.

Labrador Retrievers do well on a dog food that uses a muscle meat as the first ingredient. Muscle meats are listed on the label simply as beef, chicken, fish, and so on. Steer away from foods with a lot of soy or soy products, as these are thought to contribute to stomach gas, which can lead to bloat (for more on this disease, see chapter 8).

Many Labrador Retrievers have sensitivity to the grains used in many commercial dog foods. Cereal grains, such as rice, wheat, corn, and barley, are used in commercial dog foods because they are inexpensive. However, many dogs, including many Lab puppies, will develop a behavior problem when eating these foods. Cereal grains have a high glycemic index—they raise the dog's blood sugar. Sensitive dogs will then become fidgety, wiggly, and have a hard time concentrating and learning. These Labs would do better eating a food with carbohydrates from potatoes, sweet potatoes, apples, or bananas, because these foods help maintain a stable blood sugar level with no spikes or valleys, and these foods are more easily digested.

When you travel with your dog, bring food and water from home to avoid digestive upsets.

Homemade Diets

Dog owners who feed homemade diets usually do so because they are concerned about the quality of commercially available foods. Some owners do not want their dogs eating the additives or preservatives that are in many commercial dog foods. Others cook their dogs' food so they can control exactly what their dogs eat. Many, many people began making homemade diets for their dogs during and after the pet food recalls of 2007.

There are many resources now available to dog owners who wish to feed a homemade diet. Just make sure the diet is complete and contains all the nutrients your dog needs, and keep a line of communication open with your veterinarian so they can monitor your dog's continued good health.

Seven Mistakes to Avoid

1. Don't feed your dog chocolate, raisins, grapes, macadamia nuts, onions, or any highly spiced, greasy, or salty foods. The first five can be toxic, and spicy or junk foods can lead to an upset stomach.
2. Don't believe all the dog food advertising you see and hear. Keep in mind that advertising has one goal: to get you to buy that product.
3. If you change foods for any reason, don't do it all at once. Mix the foods so the dog has 25 percent new food and 75 percent old food for a week. Then feed half and half for a week. Finally, offer 75 percent new food and 25 percent old food for a week. This will decrease the chances of an upset stomach.
4. Nutritional changes are slow, so don't keep switching every few weeks. Feed the new food for at least six to eight weeks before evaluating the results and making any other changes.
5. Don't feed your dog from the table. This will lead to begging and even stealing.
6. Be careful about giving your Lab any bones, except raw beef knuckle-bones. Labs have powerful jaws and could crack, splinter, and swallow smaller bones, which can cause choking and damage the gastrointestinal system.
7. When traveling, don't assume your dog will be fine drinking the local tap water. On a trip, bring food and water from home to limit any digestive upsets.

Chapter 7

Grooming Your Labrador Retriever

Some dog owners seem to think grooming refers to the beauty parlor treatment Poodles go through every few weeks. That's not true. Grooming is the process of caring for the outside of your Labrador Retriever. That includes regular brushing, checking his skin and coat for problems, cleaning his ears and eyes, and trimming his toenails. Although Poodles have much more complicated care requirements, your Lab still needs—and deserves—your regular attention.

The Labrador Retriever has a double coat. The undercoat is short and dense, while the outercoat consists of harsher hairs. The combined effect is a weatherproof coat that protects the dog from rain and cold water.

The coat is relatively short, especially when compared to a Collie or an Alaskan Malamute. At the same time, it is not as short as a Boxer's or Doberman Pinscher's coat. It does shed, especially in the spring and fall. Although the Lab's coat appears to be easy to care for, and it is, it requires some care to keep it looking its best and to make sure the dog remains healthy.

Brushing

Your Lab should be brushed two to three times each week. Brushing will reduce some of the hair in the house, and that's always nice. But brushing also stimulates the oil glands in the skin, which help keep the coat healthy and shiny. There are three grooming tools you can use.

Brush your Lab two to three times a week to keep him looking his best.

Pin Brush

A pin brush looks like a woman's hairbrush. It has an oval head with numerous metal, pinlike bristles. These pins have round heads on them, like a bead. This brush will go through the coat down to the skin (and the bead on the bristle prevents scratching the skin) and will loosen clumps of coat, dirt, grass seeds, burrs, or other debris. Use this brush first.

To brush your dog, lay him on his side and sit or kneel next to him so that you and he can both relax. Then, starting at his head, begin brushing in the direction the coat grows. Brush with the coat, from the head down to the tip of the tail. Make sure the brush goes all the way through the coat to the skin; don't just skim over the top of the coat. By going through the coat to the skin, this brush will make sure the undercoat is not bunched, clumped, or stuck together. It will also pull out the dead undercoat.

When you have finished one side, then roll your dog over and do the same thing on the other side.

Slicker Brush

Not all Lab coats have the same density and texture. If your Lab has a more dense coat, the slicker brush may be a better choice. A slicker brush has many thin wire bristles that are bent at an angle. This brush is effective at getting out all the dead hair, especially from the undercoat. Use the slicker brush after the pin brush, and use it the same way you did the pin brush. Don't forget the tail!

Shedding Blade

The next tool you will use is a shedding blade. This looks like a flexible saw blade bent into a U shape with a handle holding both blades together. This does not go through the coat but, instead, will pull out all the dead outercoat. With your dog still lying on his side, repeat your previous pattern, going over the dog from head to tail on each side with the shedding blade.

Vacuum

You may also wish to introduce your dog to a canister vacuum. If he will tolerate it, it will help tremendously to get the last bits of shedding coat off the dog. When you're done brushing your Lab, you should have a dog with a clean, shiny coat and a garbage bag (or vacuum bag) full of loose hair.

Bathing

As a breed developed to be in the water often (originally to retrieve fish and birds from very cold water), Labs have an oily coat. Their skin produces these oils to keep the coat waterproof, so the dog is protected from the cold. The oils in the Lab's skin that help produce the shiny coat can also cause some problems, though. When those oils mix with dirt, they can cause the dog to smell. Most people refer to this as a "doggy smell," and that it is, but you don't have to live with it. So, depending upon your Labrador Retriever's living environment and his work and play habits, you may wish to bathe him once a week or once a month.

When choosing a shampoo, ask your veterinarian or a dog groomer for recommendations. There are many shampoos on the market. When you buy the shampoo, read

The water-repellent oils on a Lab's coat can start to smell "doggy." A bath will take away the smell.

New Products in the Fight Against Fleas

At one time, battling fleas meant exposing your dog and your-self to toxic dips, sprays, powders, and collars. But today there are flea preventives that work very well and are safe for your dog, you, and the environment. The two most common types are insect growth regulators (IGRs), which stop the immature flea from developing or maturing, and adult flea killers. To deal with an active infestation, experts usually recommend a product that has both.

These next-generation flea fighters generally come in one of two forms:

- **Topical treatments or spot-ons.** These products are applied to the skin, usually between the shoulder blades. The product is absorbed through the skin into the dog's system. Among the most widely available spot-ons are Advantage (kills adult fleas and larvae), Revolution (kills adult fleas), Frontline Plus (kills adult fleas and larvae, plus an IGR), K-9 Advantix (kills adult fleas and larvae), and BioSpot (kills adult fleas and larvae, plus an IGR).
- **Systemic products.** This is a pill your dog swallows that transmits a chemical throughout the dog's bloodstream. When a flea bites the dog, it picks up this chemical, which then prevents the flea's eggs from developing. Among the most widely available systemic products are Program (kills larvae only, plus an IGR) and Capstar (kills adult fleas).

Make sure you read all the labels and apply the products exactly as recommended, and that you check to make sure they are safe for puppies.

the label carefully. Some shampoos are made to be diluted in water, a capful or half a cup to a gallon of water. Other shampoos are formulated to use as is. Other shampoos, especially those formulated to kill fleas or ticks, must remain on the dog for two to five minutes before being rinsed off. To make sure you use the shampoo correctly, read the entire label. Don't use shampoos made for people; these are much too harsh and will dry out your Lab's skin and coat.

You can bathe your dog outside if the weather is warm and the water from your hose isn't too cold, or you can bathe him in the bathtub. Either way, change into old clothes (you will get wet!) and leash your dog. Put a cotton ball in each of his ears so you don't get water in them. Make sure he is thoroughly brushed first, then use the hose or shower to get him entirely wet. It can be hard sometimes to wet the dog clear to the skin—that wonderful double coat repels water well.

Once your Lab is wet, put some shampoo on your hands and start working it into the coat, starting at the head and ears and working down the neck. Be careful not to get soap in his eyes. Continue until the dog is covered with shampoo. Don't forget his legs, tummy, groin, and tail. Start rinsing in the same way, starting at his head and working down the body. Rinse thoroughly—any soap left on his body could make him itchy and may even cause a rash.

Once your Lab is thoroughly rinsed, let him shake off the excess water. Then, before you towel him off, go get your canister vacuum. Put the hose on the air exit port so the vacuum is blowing air instead of sucking air, and use that airstream to blow the excess water off your dog. Now towel dry him and, if you wish, use your blow-dryer to finish drying him. Just remember blow-dryers can get very hot, so be careful not to burn him with it. Never use the hottest setting.

Other Details

Keeping your Lab clean and brushed is only a small part of the body care he needs. The rest of the grooming chores can be done when you brush your dog, or you can set up a separate routine for them. Just make sure you remember to do them regularly. Don't forget!

Ears

Each time you brush your Labrador Retriever, you should check his ears for dirt and wax buildup. Because the Lab's ears are folded down (called *drop ears*), when his ears get wet, they may stay wet. Bacteria, wax, and dirt can build up and cause infections. If the dog's ears have a sour smell or seem to be extremely dirty, or if the dog is pawing at his ears or shaking his head, call your veterinarian immediately.

Each time you brush your dog, check his ears for dirt and wax.

To clean the ears, fold one earflap up over the dog's head so the ear rests on the top of his head. Dampen a cotton swab with witch hazel and gently clean out the ear, getting the swab into all the cracks and crevices of the ear. Never put anything down the dog's ear canal. You may want to use two or three cotton swabs per ear, especially if the ear is dirty. Leave the ear flap up for a moment or two so the inside of the ear can dry. Then turn the dog around and repeat on the other ear.

Eyes

If your Lab has some matter in the corners of his eyes, just use a damp paper towel to wipe it off. It's just like the sleep matter you sometimes have when you wake up. However, if your dog has a different type of discharge, or his eyes are red and irritated, call your veterinarian. Get him into the vet right away if you see a foreign object—such as a grass seed—in his eye.

Teeth

If you start when your Lab is a puppy, keeping his teeth clean can be easy. Take some gauze from your first-aid kit and wrap it around your index finger. Dampen it and dip it in baking soda. Take that baking soda and rub it over your dog's teeth, working gently over each tooth, the inside and the outside, and into the gum line, taking care not to hurt the dog.

The rubbing action of the rough gauze and the chemical characteristics of the baking soda will help prevent plaque formation and will get rid of the bacteria that form on the teeth and gums.

Do two or three teeth and let your dog have a drink. Then work on a couple more. You may even want to break it into several sessions, doing half or a quarter of the dog's mouth at each session.

Nails

Your dog's nails need to be trimmed regularly, preferably once a week. If the nails get too long, they can actually deform the foot by applying pressure against the ground, causing the toes to be pushing into an unnatural position. Long nails are more prone to breaking and tearing, too, and that can be as painful to the dog as it is when we tear a long fingernail. However, if the nails are trimmed regularly, you can keep them short and healthy.

There are two basic types of nail clippers. One is shaped much like a pair of scissors, and the other has a guillotine-type blade. The scissors-type can be found in a large size that will cut the Lab's larger nails.

With your clippers in hand, have your dog lie down on the floor in front of you. Take one foot and pull the hair back from the nail so you can see the entire

Get your puppy used to nail clipping when he is young and he won't make a fuss when he's grown up.

> **Common Sense**
>
> A healthy Labrador Retriever should have a shiny coat, clean ears, and short nails. The dog shouldn't smell or be offensive in any way. Use your common sense when grooming your dog. If you are unfamiliar with a shampoo, dip, or other grooming product, read the label. If you are worried a certain product might be too harsh or might be dangerous to you, don't use it on your dog. If you have questions, call a local groomer.

nail. If your dog's nails are black, you won't be able to see the *quick*, which is the bundle of nerves running inside the nail; but if your Labrador Retriever has one or two white nails, you will be able to see the pink quick inside. When you trim the nails, if you cut into the quick, the nail will bleed and your dog will cry. The quick is just like your nail bed and hurts just as much if it is cut. So trim the nails just beyond the quick.

If your dog has a white nail, you can use it as a guide in determining how much to trim. However, if all your dog's nails are black, you will have to take it a little slower. Look at the nail's shape. It is arched, and if the nails are long, there is a slight hook at the end. You can safely trim that hook without cutting the quick. Then, very carefully, take off just a little more.

Obviously, you will know when you hit the quick—you'll feel guilty because your dog is crying and bleeding. Don't panic. Take a bar of soap and rub the nail along the soap. The soap will clog the nail for a few minutes until the nail can clot. Now, while the soap is in the nail, hold that paw and look at the nail you cut. How far did you go? Trim the other nails using that one as a guide but taking less off the rest.

Many dogs dislike having their nails trimmed. Some will whine or cry so much you may even think you have cut into the quick. Other dogs will try to escape from you, fighting and wiggling. If your Lab dislikes nail trimming, try to make it as pleasant as possible. Have the nail clippers at hand, but hidden, perhaps in your pocket. Have your dog lie down in front of you and then give him a massage, slowly and gently. When the dog is relaxed, touch one of his feet, also slowly and gently. Then go back to massaging, then touch his feet again. By doing this, you are showing him that touching his feet is painless and is followed by more massaging.

When your dog will let you touch his paws without reacting, have the nail clippers in hand as you massage, then trim one nail. Trim just one, then go back to massaging. When he is relaxed, trim one more. And so on. If your dog is very frightened of nail trimming, you may want to break this down even further, doing one paw per massage session.

External Parasites

External parasites live on the outside of your dog's body. They are called parasites because they need your dog for life—either for food or to continue their life cycle. Without your dog, these creatures would die. Unfortunately, parasites can also cause your dog great discomfort, irritation, illness, and sometimes even death. It's very important that you keep an eye on your dog and make sure parasites stay off him.

Fleas

Fleas are about the size of the head of a pin, but the dangers these little blood-sucking pests pose to your dog are formidable. A flea is a crescent-shaped insect with six legs. It is a tremendous jumper. Fleas live by biting a host animal and drinking its blood.

You can see fleas by brushing the dog's coat against the lie of the hair and looking at the skin. A flea will appear as a tiny darting speck, trying to hide in the hair. Fleas show up best on the dog's belly, near the genitals. You can also look for them by having your dog lie on a solid-colored sheet and brushing vigorously. If you see salt-and-pepper–type residue falling to the sheet, your Lab

A heavy infestation of fleas can seriously harm a young dog.

Making Your Environment Flea Free

If there are fleas on your dog, there are fleas in your home, yard, and car, even if you can't see them. Take these steps to combat them.

In your home:

- Wash whatever is washable (the dog bed, sheets, blankets, pillow covers, slipcovers, curtains, etc.).
- Vacuum everything else in your home—furniture, floors, rugs, everything. Pay special attention to the folds and crevices in upholstery, cracks between floorboards, and the spaces between the floor and the baseboards. Flea larvae are sensitive to sunlight, so inside the house they prefer deep carpet, bedding, and cracks and crevices.
- When you're done, throw the vacuum cleaner bag away—in an outside garbage can.
- Use a nontoxic flea-killing powder, such as Flea Busters or Zodiac FleaTrol, to treat your carpets (but remember, it does not control fleas elsewhere in the house). The powder stays deep in the carpet and kills fleas (using a form of boric acid) for up to a year.
- If you have a particularly serious flea problem, consider using a fogger or long-lasting spray to kill any adult and larval fleas, or having a professional exterminator treat your home.

has fleas. The residue is made up of fecal matter (the "pepper") and eggs (the "salt").

A heavy infestation can kill a dog, especially the very young and very old. Keep in mind that each time a flea bites, it eats a drop or two of blood. Multiply numerous bites a day by the number of fleas, and you can see how dangerous an infestation can be.

Fleas' biting their host can also cause other problems. Many Labs are allergic to the flea's saliva and scratch each bite until a sore develops. This is called *flea allergy dermatitis* and is a serious problem in many areas of the country. Fleas can also carry disease, such as plague, and are the intermediary host for tapeworms, an internal parasite.

To reduce the flea population, you need to treat the dog and his environment (see the box above). If you treat only the dog and do not treat the house, yard,

In your car:

- Take out the floor mats and hose them down with a strong stream of water, then hang them up to dry in the sun.
- Wash any towels, blankets, or other bedding you regularly keep in the car.
- Thoroughly vacuum the entire interior of your car, paying special attention to the seams between the bottom and back of the seats.
- When you're done, throw the vacuum cleaner bag away—in an outside garbage can.

In your yard:

- Flea larvae prefer shaded areas that have plenty of organic material and moisture, so rake the yard thoroughly and bag all the debris in tightly sealed bags.
- Spray your yard with an insecticide that has residual activity for at least thirty days. Insecticides that use a form of boric acid are nontoxic. Some newer products contain an insect growth regulator (such as fenoxycarb) and need to be applied only once or twice a year.
- For an especially difficult flea problem, consider having an exterminator treat your yard.
- Keep your yard free of piles of leaves, weeds, and other organic debris. Be especially careful in shady, moist areas, such as under bushes.

and car, your Lab will simply become reinfested. Flea eggs can live in the environment for years, waiting for the right conditions to hatch. This is not an insect that can be ignored!

If you have any questions about what is safe to use on your dog, call your veterinarian or groomer. If you have questions about how to use a particular product, call the manufacturers. They will be more than willing to talk to you and explain exactly how the product should be used.

Ticks

As you examine your Lab for fleas, also check for ticks that may have lodged in the ears or in the hair at the base of the ear, the armpits, or around the genitals. If you find a tick, remove it as described in the box on page 74. Don't just grab and

How to Get Rid of a Tick

Although the new generation of flea fighters are partially effective in killing ticks once they are on your dog, they are not 100 percent effective and will not keep ticks from biting your dog in the first place. During tick season (which, depending on where you live, can be spring, summer, and/or fall), examine your dog every day for ticks. Pay particular attention to your dog's neck, behind the ears, the armpits, and the groin.

When you find a tick, use a pair of tweezers to grasp the tick as close as possible to the dog's skin and pull it out using firm, steady pressure. Check to make sure you get the whole tick (mouth parts left in your dog's skin can cause an infection), then wash the wound and dab on some antibiotic ointment. Watch for signs of inflammation.

Ticks carry very serious diseases that are transmittable to humans, so dispose of the tick safely. *Never* crush it between your fingers. Don't flush it down the toilet either, because the tick will survive the trip and infect another animal. Instead, use the tweezers to place the tick in a tight-sealing jar or plastic dish with a little alcohol, put on the lid, and dispose of the container in an outdoor garbage can. Wash the tweezers thoroughly with hot water and alcohol.

pull or the tick's head may separate from the body. If the head remains in the skin, an infection or abscess may result, and veterinary treatment may be required.

A word of caution: Don't use your fingers or fingernails to pull out ticks. Ticks can carry a number of diseases, including Lyme disease, Rocky Mountain spotted fever, and several others, all of which can be very serious for both dogs and humans. A couple of weeks after removing ticks from her dogs (using her fingers), a friend of mine came down with viral encephalitis, a serious disease. After quizzing her, her doctor believed she got the disease from the ticks. Fortunately, she is now okay, but a pair of tweezers would have saved her and her husband a lot of pain and worry.

Whenever you've been out in woods or fields with your dog, check him carefully for ticks.

Although some flea products are advertised as being able to kill ticks, too, the best way to make sure your Lab is tick-free is to examine his body regularly. Make it part of a daily exam.

Mites

Mites are tiny creatures. Experts say we all have them—humans, canines, and all other creatures, including the ones who live in the ocean. The mites that infest your dog usually do so without causing a problem. However, when the dog is stressed or his immune system is threatened, sometimes the mites can proliferate out of control. Some dogs may also have sensitivities to mites.

Sarcoptic mange is caused by a mite that bites your dog. Your Lab will itch, scratch horribly, and you will see tiny red bumps and patchy, crusty areas on his body, legs, and stomach. Your veterinarian will need to treat him, but this condition usually responds very well to treatment.

Demodectic mange is caused by a different mite. Often dogs with this do not itch and sometimes act as if there is no problem at all. The first spots usually show up on the dog's face as small, moth-eaten–looking spots where the hair is missing. Again, the veterinarian needs to treat this mite infestation.

Chapter 8

Keeping Your Labrador Retriever Healthy

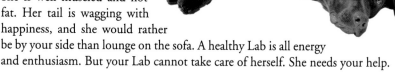

A healthy Lab has bright eyes and a shiny coat and is always ready to play. She is well muscled and not fat. Her tail is wagging with happiness, and she would rather be by your side than lounge on the sofa. A healthy Lab is all energy and enthusiasm. But your Lab cannot take care of herself. She needs your help.

Preventive Health Care

The easiest way to make sure your dog is well cared for is to set up a routine, then follow this routine each and every day without fail. Without a routine, it's too easy to say to yourself, "I had a tough day at work today, I'll do that tomorrow." Eventually, if you procrastinate enough, you'll forget what you were going to do. Your dog is the one who will suffer.

The Daily Inspection

Once a day, you need to run your hands over your Lab—not just over the coat as you would do when you pet your dog, but run your fingers through and under the coat so you can feel the dog's skin. As you do this, you will get to know the feel of your dog. Then if a tick latches on and buries its head in your dog's skin, you will feel it with your fingers. If your dog cuts herself, or has a lump or bruise or a skin rash, you will feel it. By checking the dog like this everyday, you will find these things before they turn into bigger problems.

After you finish brushing your dog, put the brushes down, and starting at the dog's head again, run your hands over your dog's head, around the muzzle, over the skull, feeling around the base of the ears, through the thick neck hair, making sure you touch every square inch of skin. Take your time as you do this. Think of it as giving your dog a gentle massage. Your dog may go to sleep as you massage, but make sure you don't. Stay alert and look for problems.

As you massage and examine your Lab, become familiar with every part of her body. Let your hands and fingers learn what your dog feels like. Run your hands over the shoulders, down the front legs, over the ribcage, and down the back to the hips. Run your hands down each leg, handling each toe on each paw, checking for burrs and foxtails, cuts and scratches. Don't forget to run your hands down the tail, too, checking for lumps, bumps, and burrs.

A side benefit of this daily exam will show up when you need to take your Lab to the veterinarian. Your dog will be used to intimate handling and will not be as stressed by it as a dog who is not handled in this manner.

Check the Ears, Teeth, and Skin

In chapter 7, we discuss how to clean your Lab's teeth during your regular grooming sessions. It is also important to check her teeth regularly, looking for

Get in the habit of giving your dog a daily exam and massage. You can make it a game or a special cuddle time.

Vaccines

What vaccines dogs need and how often they need them has been a subject of controversy for several years. Researchers, healthcare professionals, vaccine manufacturers, and dog owners do not always agree on which vaccines each dog needs or how often booster shots must be given.

In 2006, the American Animal Hospital Association issued a set of vaccination guidelines and recommendations intended to help dog owners and veterinarians sort through much of the controversy and conflicting information. The guidelines designate four vaccines as *core*, or essential, for every dog, because of the serious nature of the diseases and their widespread distribution. These are canine distemper virus (using a modified live virus or recombinant modified live virus vaccine), canine parvovirus (using a modified live virus vaccine), canine adenovirus-2 (using a modified live virus vaccine), and rabies (using a killed virus). The general recommendations for their administration (except rabies, for which you must follow local laws) are:

- Vaccinate puppies at 6–8 weeks, 9–11 weeks, and 12–14 weeks.
- Give an initial "adult" vaccination when the dog is older than 16 weeks; two doses, three to four weeks apart, are

inflamed gums, foreign objects, and cracked or broken teeth. So as you massage your dog's head, open her mouth and take a look. Look at the inside surfaces of the teeth and the outside surfaces. Become familiar with what the teeth look like so you will spot any problems.

In chapter 7, we also talk about how to clean the inside of the ears. As you wipe out each ear, check for scratches or foreign objects and give the ear a sniff. If there is quite a bit of discharge and the ear has a sour smell, call your veterinarian.

Skin allergies are not uncommon in this breed. Skin allergies can show up as red skin, a rash, hives, or a weeping, oozing sore. If during your daily exam you advised, but one dose is considered protective and acceptable.

- Give a booster shot when the dog is 1 year old.
- Give a subsequent booster shot every three years, unless there are risk factors that make it necessary to vaccinate more or less often.

Noncore vaccines should only be considered for those dogs who risk exposure to a particular disease because of geographic area, lifestyle, frequency of travel, or other issues. They include vaccines against distemper-measles virus, canine parainfluenza virus, leptospirosis, Bordetella bronchiseptica, and Borrelia burgdorferi (Lyme disease).

Vaccines that are not generally recommended because the disease poses little risk to dogs or is easily treatable, or the vaccine has not been proven to be effective, are those against giardia, canine coronavirus, and canine adenovirus-1.

Often, combination injections are given to puppies, with one shot containing several core and noncore vaccines. Your veterinarian may be reluctant to use separate shots that do not include the noncore vaccines, because they must be specially ordered. If you are concerned about these noncore vaccines, talk to your vet.

see a skin problem developing, get your Lab in to your veterinarian right away. It's much easier to treat a skin problem when it's first starting than it is later when the problem has spread and the dog is tormented by the itching. Your veterinarian might also be able to help you identify the cause of the sensitivity.

During your daily exam, check also for cuts, scrapes, bruises, and sores. If you find any minor cuts and scrapes, you can wash them with soap and water and apply a mild antibiotic ointment. However, if a cut is gaping or looks red and inflamed, call your veterinarian.

Problems That Affect the Lab

Unfortunately, there are several health problems that affect many Labrador Retrievers. That doesn't mean every Lab has these problems, but they do have a tendency to show up in the breed. It's very important that when you choose your new dog, you discuss these health problems with the breeder. Ideally, they have tested all of their breeding animals before breeding. Your veterinarian should also be aware of these disorders, not just so they can be diagnosed, but also so they can keep up on the newest treatments.

Bloat

Bloat, or gastric torsion, is the acute dilation of the stomach, caused when the stomach fills with gas and air and, as a result, swells. This swelling prevents the dog from vomiting or passing gas. Consequently, the pressure builds, cutting off blood from the heart and to other parts of the body. This causes shock or heart failure, either of which can cause death. Bloat can also cause torsion, where the stomach turns on its long axis, again causing death.

The first symptoms of bloat are obvious. The dog will be pacing or panting, showing signs of distress. The dog's sides will begin to distend. To be successful, treatment should begin at once—there is no time to waste. If the pressure is not immediately relieved, death can follow within an hour. Get your dog to the nearest veterinary emergency clinic.

To prevent bloat, do not allow your Lab to drink large quantities of water after exercising or after eating. Feed two smaller meals each day instead of one large meal, and limit exercise after eating until a couple of hours have passed. Feed a good-quality food, preferably one that does not expand significantly when wet and does not produce large quantities of gas.

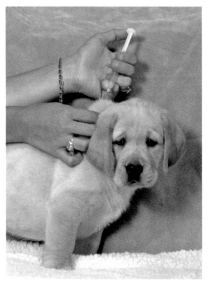

What vaccines a dog needs depends on the individual dog. Discuss a vaccination plan with your veterinarian.

To see how much your dog's food expands, or to see how much gas the food produces, take a handful of the kibble and drop it in a bowl of warm water. After fifteen minutes, look at the food. Some foods will be wet but will not enlarge. This is good. Other foods will triple their size when wet. This can be dangerous if it happens in your dog's stomach. Some foods will be producing gas bubbles, almost as if they were carbonated. Again, this can be bad news in your dog's stomach.

Cancer

Unfortunately, some Lab bloodlines seem to be prone to cancer. Cancer in dogs, just as in people, is not one disease but a variety of diseases. Although research is continuing, it is unknown how or why some cells go on a rampage and become cancerous.

Bloat tends to affect large dogs with big chests. It is a serious emergency.

When you examine your Lab each day, be aware of any lumps or bumps you might feel, especially as your dog is growing older. Your veterinarian can biopsy any suspicious lump, and if it is cancer, many times it can be removed. Early removal offers the best chance of success. Unfortunately, cancer is often fatal.

Cold Water Tail

It has been reported that after a day or two of heavy hunting, with the obvious excitement resulting in strong tail wagging by the dog, along with repeated exposure to cold water, the muscles at the base of the tail swell. This strange-sounding disorder really isn't that uncommon, especially in the hunting Lab community. Experts are still looking at the condition to see if the muscles alone are involved or whether the swelling of the muscles presses on nerves.

In any case, when it occurs, the tail hangs limp and the dog appears to be in discomfort. With rest and anti-inflammatory medications, the dog recovers.

Dwarfism

There are two types of dwarfism seen in Labs. The first is associated with retinal dysplasia (see page 86). In this form of dwarfism, the dog may have vision problems or blindness from the retinal dysplasia and have skeletal problems as well.

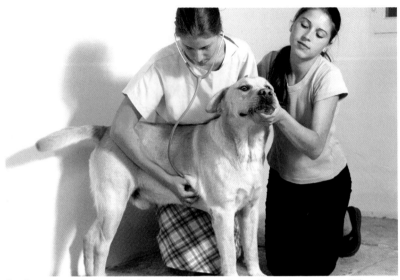

Regular veterinary checkups will help you detect health problems early on, when many can still be treated.

The dog's head is usually larger than normal and the legs are short and bowed outwards. The dog will have a Bulldog-type appearance.

The second type of dwarfism is thought to be caused by a decrease in growth hormones produced by the pituitary gland. As a result, the dog does not grow correctly. These dogs appear to be in proportion with no skeletal deformities, but just remain very small. In addition, the coat may be softer than it should be and woolly, and the dog may develop hair loss.

Any dogs showing any symptoms of dwarfism should be spayed or neutered, and the breeder needs to be informed so they can take another look at their breeding program.

Elbow Dysplasia

Elbow dysplasia is thought to be due to the incorrect development of the three bones that make up the elbow. The affected elbow can be painful, inhibit movement, and can develop arthritis.

Epilepsy

Epilepsy (a seizure disorder) can occur in Labrador Retrievers. Idiopathic epilepsy (the form of epilepsy that is not caused by a brain tumor, injury, or other obvious cause) tends to be inherited and usually appears between the ages of 1 and 3 years, although it may first appear up to about 7 years of age. The intensity of the seizures can vary, from mild twitches and a dazed look in the eyes to full convulsions. Managing epilepsy will require a close partnership with your veterinarian.

Exercise-Induced Collapse

This disorder usually appears in dogs between the ages of 7 months and 2 years. The dog can usually play just fine, but after about five to twenty minutes of heavy exercise or hard training (as with field training), she begins to appear stiff. The rear legs become weak and often collapse. In some cases, the forelegs also become weak and unable to support the dog's weight. The dog may appear to be disoriented. Some dogs die.

This disorder is still being studied. Because littermates may all show signs of the disorder, it is currently thought to be inherited. Treatments vary, as do the dog's ability to recover. If a Lab shows signs of this disorder during strenuous exercise, all exercise should stop immediately, and the dog should be taken to the veterinarian.

Hip Dysplasia

Hip dysplasia is a failure of the head of the femur (thighbone) to fit into the acetabulum (hip socket). Hip dysplasia is not just caused by poorly formed or malpositioned bones; many researchers believe the muscles and tendons in the leg and hip may also play a part.

Hip dysplasia is considered a polygenic inherited disorder, which means many different genes may lead to the disease. Also, environmental factors may contribute to the development of hip dysplasia, including nutrition and exercise, although the part environmental factors play in the disease is highly debated among experts.

Hip dysplasia can cause a wide range of problems, from mild lameness to movement irregularities to crippling pain. Dogs with hip dysplasia must often limit their activities, may need corrective surgery, or may even need to be euthanized because of the pain.

Contrary to popular belief, hip dysplasia cannot be diagnosed by watching a dog run or by the way

Swimming is an excellent way to exercise dogs with joint problems.

Sometimes the only sign that a dog is ill is that her behavior is not quite right. Get to know what is normal for your dog, and call your veterinarian if you see any changes.

she lies down. It can only be diagnosed accurately by special X-ray. Once the X-ray is taken, it can be sent to the Orthopedic Foundation for Animals (OFA) or the University of Pennsylvania Hip Improvement Program (PennHIP), which reads, grades, and certifies the X-rays of dogs over the age of 2 years. Sound hips are rated excellent, good, or fair, and the dog's owner receives a certificate with the rating. A dysplastic dog will be rated as mild, moderate, or severe. Any dog who is found to be dysplastic should be removed from any breeding program and spayed or neutered.

Hypothyroidism

The thyroid gland produces hormones that govern or affect a number of bodily functions. A dog with hypothyroid is producing fewer hormones than she should. She may show symptoms ranging from infertility to dry, dull coat, flaky skin, runny eyes, or even difficulty walking. Thyroid problems can be diagnosed with a blood test, and medication can usually relieve the symptoms fairly rapidly. In most cases, the dog will have to remain on the medication for life.

Lick Granuloma

A lick granuloma is an injury the dog does to herself. She begins to lick at a spot on one of her legs—usually a front leg around the ankle, but it may also be a rear leg right above the paw—and she continues licking, producing a wet, weepy sore that often becomes infected. This compulsive behavior has been associated with boredom and separation anxiety. Curing the problem often requires the help of a veterinarian and a behaviorist.

Megaesophagus

This disorder is caused by a lack of peristaltic function in the esophagus. In other words, the muscular contractions of the esophagus that move food down into the stomach are not happening as they should. Food then builds up in the esophagus, causing it to stretch, until the food empties into the stomach by sheer pressure, or the dog vomits the food back up.

Experts feel this is an inherited problem, and dogs with the condition should be spayed or neutered. Treatment includes feeding the dog several small meals throughout the day from a raised (shoulder-height) platform.

Muscle Myopathy

This disorder usually appears in puppies between 3 and 6 months of age. The puppies will be less inclined to play and will be sore when touched. The muscles gradually waste away until the dog looks lean and lanky instead of stocky. Heat and cold both seem to cause more discomfort, as does strenuous exercise.

This is an inherited disorder. Dogs developing it should be spayed or neutered, as should the parents of the dog who developed it. There is no cure or treatment.

Obesity

As we discussed earlier in the book, Labs can be prone to obesity. A dog who weighs more than she should can develop diabetes, hypothyroidism, and back, shoulder, and other skeletal problems. Although the breed does tend to gain weight easily, obesity is caused by too many calories and not enough exercise.

Obesity can cause a host of other health problems. Keep your dog at a healthy weight.

Osteochondritis Dissecans (OCD)

OCD occurs most often in young, fast-growing puppies of larger breeds, including Labs. The bone underlying the cartilage in joints breaks down, causing the puppy pain. It can happen in the elbow, shoulder, or ankle. Contributing factors include obesity, repetitive motions (such as running long distances), or jumping off high places or jumping over high jumps.

Panosteitis

This disease causes lameness and pain in young, rapidly growing puppies, usually between the ages of 6 and 14 months, although it is occasionally seen up to 18 months of age. The lameness usually affects one leg at a time and can sporadically move from one leg to another. Some veterinarians prescribe aspirin to relieve the pain, and most suggest the dog be kept quiet. Often, this problem clears up on its own.

Many experts feel the tendency to develop this disorder is inherited, but it can also be made worse by feeding a diet that is not balanced—perhaps too high in carbohydrates or too much protein without enough carbohydrates. The debate continues, so talk to your dog's breeder or veterinarian about diet and panosteitis.

PRA and Other Eye Disorders

Labs are, unfortunately, at risk for several eye disorders, including progressive retinal atrophy (PRA), cataracts, and retinal dysplasia. With PRA there is a progressive deterioration of the retina. Gradually the dog becomes blind. This is thought to be inherited, and all dogs who develop symptoms should be removed from a breeding program. Unfortunately, this problem usually shows up between 4 to 6 years of age, so some affected dogs may have already been used for breeding.

Cataracts cause cloudiness in the lens of the eye, and severe cataracts can cause blindness. Cataracts that develop early in the dog's life are almost always inherited, while those that appear in dogs who are 10 years of age or older are usually due to old age. Some cataracts can be removed, so talk to your veterinarian when signs of cloudiness first appear.

Retinal dysplasia is an abnormal development of the retina. In mild cases the vision is only slightly affected, but in more severe cases the dog is blind. This disease is often associated with Labs who carry the genes for dwarfism.

Internal Parasites

External parasites live on the outside of your Lab's body and are discussed in chapter 7. Internal parasites live inside, and you may not see any signs of an infestation until it has progressed.

Roundworms

These long white worms are the most commonly found internal parasites, especially in puppies, although they occasionally infest adult dogs and people. The adult female roundworm can lay up to 200,000 eggs a day, which are passed in the dog's feces. Roundworms can be transmitted only via the feces. Because of this, stools should be picked up daily, and your dog should be prevented from investigating other dogs' feces.

If treated early, roundworms are not serious. However, a heavy infestation can severely affect a dog's health. Puppies with roundworms will not thrive and will appear thin, with a dull coat and potbelly. In people, roundworms can be more serious. Therefore, early treatment, regular fecal checks, and good sanitation are important, both for your Lab's continued good health and yours.

Just about all puppies get worms. Work with your veterinarian to keep your puppy free of parasites.

Hookworms

Hookworms live their adult lives in the small intestines of dogs and other animals. They attach to the intestinal wall and suck blood. When they detach and move to a new location, the old wound continues to bleed because of the anticoagulant the worm injects when it bites. Because of this, bloody diarrhea is usually the first sign of a problem.

Hookworm eggs are passed through the feces. Either they are picked up from the stools, as with roundworms, or, if conditions are right, they hatch in the soil and attach themselves to the feet of their new hosts, where they can burrow through the skin. They then migrate to the intestinal tract, where the cycle starts all over again.

People can pick up hookworms by walking barefoot in infected soil. In the Sunbelt states, children often pick up hookworm eggs when playing outside in the dirt or in a sandbox. Treatment, for both dogs and people, may have to be repeated.

Tapeworms

Tapeworms attach to the intestinal wall to absorb nutrients. They grow by creating new segments, and usually the first sign of an infestation is the ricelike segments found in the stools or on the dog's coat near the rectum. Tapeworms are acquired when a dog chews a flea bite and swallows a flea, the intermediate host. Therefore, a good flea control program (see chapter 7) is the best way to prevent a tapeworm infestation.

Whipworms

Adult whipworms live in the large intestines, where they feed on blood. The eggs are passed in the stool and can live in the soil for many years. If your dog eats the fresh spring grass or buries her bone in the yard, she can pick up eggs from the infected soil. If you garden, you could pick up eggs under your fingernails, infecting yourself if you touch your face.

Heavy infestations cause diarrhea, often watery or bloody. The dog may appear thin and anemic, with a poor coat. Severe bowel problems may result. Unfortunately, whipworms can be difficult to detect, as the worms do not continually shed eggs. Therefore, a stool sample may be clear one day and the next day show eggs.

Giardia

Giardia is common in wild animals in many areas, so if you take your Lab hiking, camping, or herding and drink out of the local spring or stream, she can pick up giardia, just as you can. Diarrhea is one of the first symptoms. If your dog has diarrhea and you and your dog have been out camping, make sure you tell your veterinarian.

Heartworms

Adult heartworms live in the upper heart and greater pulmonary arteries, where they damage the vessel walls. Poor circulation results, which causes damage to other bodily functions. Eventually, death from heart failure results.

The adult worms produce thousands of tiny larvae called *microfilaria*. These circulate throughout the bloodstream until they are sucked up by an intermediate host, a mosquito. The microfilaria go through the larval stages in the mosquito, then are transferred back to another dog when the mosquito bites again.

Dogs infected with heartworms can be treated if caught early. Unfortunately, the treatment itself can be risky and has killed some dogs. However, preventive medications are available that kill the larvae. Heartworm can be diagnosed by a blood test, and a negative result is required before starting the preventive.

There is no way to breed a dog who is exactly like any other dog.

Why Spay and Neuter?

Breeding dogs is a serious undertaking that should only be part of a well-planned breeding program. Why? Because dogs pass on their physical and behavioral problems to their offspring. Even healthy, well-behaved dogs can pass on problems in their genes.

Is your dog so sweet that you'd like to have a litter of puppies just like her? If you breed her to another dog, the pups will not have the same genetic heritage she has. Breeding her *parents* again will increase the odds of a similar pup, but even then, the puppies in the second litter could inherit different genes. In fact, *there is no way to breed a dog to be just like another dog.*

Meanwhile, thousands and thousands of dogs are killed in animal shelters every year simply because they have no homes. Casual breeding is a big contributor to this problem.

If you don't plan to breed your dog, is it still a good idea to spay her or neuter him? Yes!

When you spay your female:

- You avoid her heat cycles, during which she discharges blood and scent.
- It greatly reduces the risk of mammary cancer and eliminates the risk of *pyometra* (an often fatal infection of the uterus) and uterine cancer.
- It prevents unwanted pregnancies.
- It reduces dominance behaviors and aggression.

When you neuter your male:

- It curbs the desire to roam and to fight with other males.
- It greatly reduces the risk of prostate cancer and eliminates the risk of testicular cancer.
- It helps reduce leg lifting and mounting behavior.
- It reduces dominance behaviors and aggression.

Emergency First Aid

Your dog cannot tell you, "I have a pain right here, and I feel like I'm going to throw up." But you should be able to recognize signs that something is not right. When you are trying to decide what is wrong with your Lab, you will need to be observant and play detective. If you call your veterinarian, they will also ask you some questions, and you need to be able to answer those.

- What caused you to think there is a problem?
- What was your first clue there's something wrong?
- Is your dog eating normally?
- What do her stools look like?
- Is the dog limping?
- When you do a hands-on exam, is the dog sore anywhere?
- Does she have a lump?
- Is anything red or swollen?

Write down all your answers before you call your veterinarian. Your vet will also ask you if your dog has a fever. You can take your dog's temperature using a rectal thermometer. Shake the thermometer down and then put some petroleum jelly on it. Using the dog's tail as a guide, insert the thermometer into the anus about an inch. Keep holding the thermometer, don't let go of it, and watch your clock. After three minutes (digital thermometers will be faster), withdraw the thermometer, wipe it off, and read the temperature. Normal is 101 to 102 degrees Fahrenheit.

The veterinarian will also ask if your dog has been vomiting and if so, what did the vomit look like? Was there anything unusual in it? Did the dog vomit up garbage? a plastic bag? grass? How often did the dog vomit—just once or is it ongoing?

Similar questions will be asked about the dog's bowel movements. Did the dog have a bowel movement? If so, did it look normal? Was there mucus or blood in the stool? Did the stool have a different or peculiar smell? Did you see any foreign objects in the stool?

Your dog depends on you to know what to do in an emergency.

How to Make a Canine First-Aid Kit

If your dog hurts herself, even a minor cut, it can be very upsetting for both of you. Having a first-aid kit handy will help you to help her, calmly and efficiently. What should be in your canine first-aid kit?

- Antibiotic ointment
- Antiseptic and antibacterial cleansing wipes
- Benadryl
- Cotton-tipped applicators
- Disposable razor
- Elastic wrap bandages
- Extra leash and collar
- First-aid tape of various widths
- Gauze bandage roll
- Gauze pads of different sizes, including eye pads
- Hydrogen peroxide
- Instant cold compress
- Kaopectate tablets or liquid
- Latex gloves
- Lubricating jelly
- Muzzle
- Nail clippers
- Pen, pencil, and paper for notes and directions
- Pepto-Bismol
- Round-ended scissors and pointy scissors
- Safety pins
- Sterile saline eyewash
- Thermometer (rectal)
- Tweezers

Be prepared to answer all these questions, and if you are nervous or scared, write them down.

It is often difficult for dog owners to decide when to call the veterinarian and when they can handle a problem at home. Listed in this section are some commonly seen problems and some basic advice on how to handle them. You'll also find advice on when to call the vet in the box on pages 94–95. However, the cost of a telephone call is small compared to your dog's life. When in doubt—call!

Your dog can get stung or bitten by an insect anytime she's outside. Many dogs are allergic to bee stings.

Animal Bites

Muzzle your dog if she is in pain. Using a pair of panty hose or a long piece of gauze, wrap it around the dog's muzzle, crossing under the jaw, then pulling it around her head, tying it in the back.

Trim the hair from around the wound and liberally pour plain water over it to flush it out. Use antibacterial wipes to clean it. A handheld pressure bandage can help stop the bleeding. Stitches may be necessary if the bite is a rip or tear, so call your vet. They may also recommend putting the dog on antibiotics.

Bee Stings

Many dogs are allergic to bee stings and will immediately start to swell. Call your vet immediately. They may recommend you give the dog an antihistamine such as Benadryl and will instruct you on the dosage. With the introduction of African bees, many bees today are more aggressive, and the chance of your dog being stung multiple times is increased. The stingers are hard to see in the Lab's coat, so use your fingers to feel for them or the swollen lumps left behind.

Bleeding

Muzzle your dog if she is in pain. Place a gauze pad or, if that is not available, a clean cloth over the

> **TIP**
>
> Tourniquets are no longer recommended, as they can cause more problems than they solve.

When to Call the Veterinarian

Go to the vet right away or take your dog to an emergency veterinary clinic if:

- Your dog is choking
- Your dog is having trouble breathing
- Your dog has been injured and you cannot stop the bleeding within a few minutes
- Your dog has been stung or bitten by an insect and the site is swelling
- Your dog has been bitten by a snake
- Your dog has been bitten by another animal (including a dog) and shows any swelling or bleeding
- Your dog has touched, licked, or in any way been exposed to a poison
- Your dog has been burned by either heat or caustic chemicals
- Your dog has been hit by a car
- Your dog has any obvious broken bones or cannot put any weight on one of her limbs
- Your dog has a seizure

Make an appointment to see the vet as soon as possible if:

- Your dog has been bitten by a cat, another dog, or a wild animal
- Your dog has been injured and is still limping an hour later

wound and apply pressure. If the wound will require stitches or if the bleeding doesn't stop, call your vet.

Choking

If your Lab is pawing at her mouth, gagging, coughing, or drooling, she may have something caught in her mouth or throat. Open her jaws and shine a flashlight down the throat. If you can see the object, reach in and pull it out, using your fingers, tweezers, or a pair of pliers. If you cannot see anything and your dog is still choking, hit her behind the neck between the shoulders to try to dislodge the object. If this fails, use an adapted Heimlich maneuver. Grasp either side of the dog's ribcage and squeeze. Don't break the ribs, but try to make a sharp enough movement to cause the air in the lungs to force the object out.

- Your dog has unexplained swelling or redness
- Your dog's appetite changes
- Your dog vomits repeatedly and can't seem to keep food down, or drools excessively while eating
- You see any changes in your dog's urination or defecation (pain during elimination, change in regular habits, blood in urine or stool, diarrhea, foul-smelling stool)
- Your dog scoots her rear end on the floor
- Your dog's energy level, attitude, or behavior changes for no apparent reason
- Your dog has crusty or cloudy eyes, or excessive tearing or discharge
- Your dog's nose is dry or chapped, hot, crusty, or runny
- Your dog's ears smell foul, have a dark discharge, or seem excessively waxy
- Your dog's gums are inflamed or bleeding, her teeth look brown, or her breath is foul
- Your dog's skin is red, flaky, itchy, or inflamed, or she keeps chewing at certain spots
- Your dog's coat is dull, dry, brittle, or bare in spots
- Your dog's paws are red, swollen, tender, cracked, or the nails are split or too long
- Your dog is panting excessively, wheezing, unable to catch her breath, breathing heavily, or sounds strange when she breathes

If your dog can breathe around the object, get to the vet as soon as possible. If your dog cannot breathe around the object, you don't have time to move the dog. Keep working on getting the object out.

Fractures

Because your Lab will be in great pain if she has broken a bone, you should muzzle her immediately. Do not try to set the fracture, but do try to immobilize the limb, if possible, by using a piece of wood and then wrapping it with gauze or soft cloth. If there is a door or board handy, use it as a backboard or stretcher so the injured limb is stable. Transport the dog to the vet as soon as possible.

Use common sense when exercising your dog in the summer months. Go out with her at dusk and dawn, when it's not as hot, or take her to the water.

Overheating or Heatstroke

Overheating or heatstroke is characterized by rapid or difficult breathing, vomiting, and even collapse. If your dog has these symptoms, you need to act at once—this can be life threatening. Immediately place your Lab in a tub of cool water or, if a tub is not available, run water from a hose over your dog. Use a rectal thermometer to take the dog's temperature and call your veterinarian immediately. Encourage your dog to drink some cool water. Transport the dog to the vet as soon as you can, or as soon as the vet recommends it.

Poisoning

Symptoms of poisoning include retching and vomiting, diarrhea, salivation, labored breathing, dilated pupils, weakness, collapse, and convulsions. Sometimes one or more symptoms will appear together, depending upon the poison. If you suspect your dog has been in contact with a poison, time is critical. Call your veterinarian right away. If your vet is not immediately available, call the ASPCA Animal Poison Control Center (see the box on page 97). The hotline and your vet can better treat your dog if you can tell them what was ingested and approximately how much.

> **TIP**
>
> Important! Do not make your dog vomit unless instructed to do so.

ASPCA Animal Poison Control Center

The ASPCA Animal Poison Control Center has a staff of licensed veterinarians and board-certified toxicologists available 24 hours a day, 365 days a year. The number to call is (888) 426-4435. You will be charged a consultation fee of $60 per case, charged to most major credit cards. There is no charge for follow-up calls in critical cases. At your request, they will also contact your veterinarian. Specific treatment and information can be provided via fax. Put the number in large, legible print with your other emergency telephone numbers. Be prepared to give your name, address, and phone number; what your dog has gotten into (the amount and how long ago); your dog's breed, age, sex, and weight; and what signs and symptoms the dog is showing. You can log onto www.aspca.org and click on "Animal Poison Control Center" for more information, including a list of toxic and nontoxic plants.

Snakebite

Without getting bitten yourself, try to get a look at the snake, making note of colors, patterns, and markings so you or your vet can identify the snake. Keep the dog as quiet as possible to restrict the flow of venom. *Do not cut X's above the wound.* That often causes more tissue damage than the bite itself, and is not known to be effective.

If your dog is in pain or is frantic, muzzle her. Call your vet immediately so that they can get some antivenom medication ready for your dog's arrival.

Torn Nails

A ripped or broken toenail can be very painful. If the dog is frantic, muzzle her to protect yourself. If a piece of the nail is hanging, trim it off. Run hydrogen peroxide over the nail. If the nail is bleeding, run it over a soft bar of soap. The soap will help the nail clot. If the quick is showing or if the nail has broken off under the skin, call your veterinarian. Antibiotics might be needed to prevent an infection.

As Your Lab Grows Older

Labs can, on average, live 12 to 14 years. However, to live that long and remain happy and healthy, your Lab will need your help. Aging in dogs, as in people, brings some changes and problems. You will see your dog's vision dim, her hearing fade, and her joints stiffen. Heart and kidney disease are common in older dogs. Reflexes will not be as sharp as they once were, and your dog may be more sensitive to heat and cold. Your dog may also get grouchy, showing less tolerance to younger dogs, to children, and to things that may not be part of her normal routine.

An old dog who has lived her life with you is a special gift. Your old Lab knows your ways, your likes and dislikes, and your habits. She almost seems able to read your mind, and her greatest joy is simply to be close to you. Your old Lab may not be able to do the work she did when she was younger, but she can still be a wonderful companion.

Arthritis is common in old dogs. The joints get stiff, especially when it's chilly. Your Lab may have trouble jumping or getting up in the morning. Give your old dog something soft to sleep on and keep her warm. Talk to your veterinarian about treatment; there are pain relievers that can help.

As your dog's activity level slows down, she will need to consume fewer calories. However, some old dogs have a problem digesting foods, too, and this may

While pups and adults love to play in the snow, older dogs are less tolerant of the cold.

show up in poor stools and a dull coat. A heaping tablespoon of yogurt with active cultures will aid her digestion.

Your Lab may need to have her teeth cleaned professionally, and this is something you should not put off doing. Bacteria that build up on the teeth can infect the gums, get into the bloodstream, and cause infections in other parts of the body, including the kidneys and heart.

Exercise is still important to your older Lab. Your dog needs the stimulation of walking around and seeing and smelling the world. Tailor the exercise to your dog's abilities and needs. If your dog can still chase a tennis ball, great! If she likes to swim, even better. However, as your dog ages, a slow walk about the neighborhood might be enough.

A well-loved dog will return your investment a thousandfold.

When It's Time to Say Good-bye

We have the option, with our dogs, not to let them suffer when they are old, ill, and infirm. There will be a time when you will need to decide how you are going to handle putting your dog out of her pain. Some feel the time has come when the dog is no longer enjoying life, when she's incontinent and despondent. Only you can make the decision, but spare your companion the humiliation of incontinence, convulsions, or the inability to stand up or move around.

If your Lab must be helped to her death, your veterinarian can give an injection that is an overdose of anesthetic. Your dog will go to sleep and quietly stop breathing. Be there with your dog. Let your arms hold your old friend and let your dog hear your voice saying how much you love her as she goes to sleep. There will be no fear, and the last thing your dog will remember is your love.

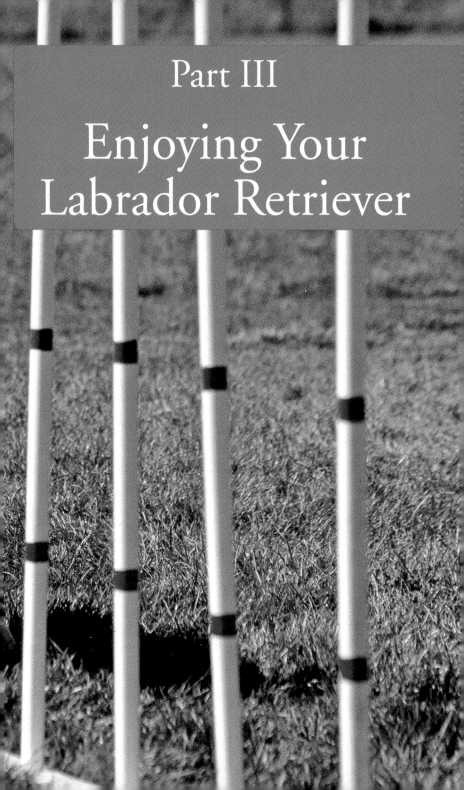

Part III

Enjoying Your Labrador Retriever

Chapter 9

Training Your Labrador Retriever

by Peggy Moran

Training makes your best friend better! A properly trained dog has a happier life and a longer life expectancy. He is also more appreciated by the people he encounters each day, both at home and out and about.

A trained dog walks nicely and joins his family often, going places untrained dogs cannot go. He is never rude or unruly, and he always happily comes when called. When he meets people for the first time, he greets them by sitting and waiting to be petted, rather than jumping up. At home he doesn't compete with his human family, and alone he is not destructive or overly anxious. He isn't continually nagged with words like "no," since he has learned not to misbehave in the first place. He is never shamed, harshly punished, or treated unkindly, and he is a well-loved, involved member of the family.

Sounds good, doesn't it? If you are willing to invest some time, thought, and patience, the words above could soon be used to describe your dog (though perhaps changing "he" to "she"). Educating your pet in a positive way is fun and easy, and there is no better gift you can give your pet than the guarantee of improved understanding and a great relationship.

This chapter will explain how to offer kind leadership, reshape your pet's behavior in a positive and practical way, and even get a head start on simple obedience training.

Understanding Builds the Bond

Dog training is a learning adventure on both ends of the leash. Before attempting to teach their dog new behaviors or change unwanted ones, thoughtful dog owners take the time to understand why their pets behave the way they do, and how their own behavior can be either a positive or negative influence on their dog.

Canine Nature

Loving dogs as much as we do, it's easy to forget they are a completely different species. Despite sharing our homes and living as appreciated members of our families, dogs do not think or learn exactly the same way people do. Even if you love your dog like a child, you must remember to respect the fact that he is actually a dog.

Dogs have no idea when their behavior is inappropriate from a human perspective. They are not aware of the value of possessions they chew or of messes they make or the worry they sometimes seem to cause. While people tend to look at behavior as good and bad or right and wrong, dogs just discover what works and what doesn't work. Then they behave accordingly, learning from their own experiences and increasing or reducing behaviors to improve results for themselves.

You might wonder, "But don't dogs want to please us"? My answer is yes, provided your pleasure reflects back to them in positive ways they can feel and appreciate. Dogs do things for *dog* reasons, and everything they do works for them in some way or they wouldn't be doing it!

The Social Dog

Our pets descended from animals who lived in tightly knit, cooperative social groups. Though far removed in appearance and lifestyle from their ancestors, our dogs still relate in many of the same ways their wild relatives did. And in their relationships with one another, wild canids either lead or follow.

Canine ranking relationships are not about cruelty and power; they are about achievement and abilities. Competent dogs with high levels of drive and confidence step up, while deferring dogs step aside. But followers don't get the short end of the stick; they benefit from the security of having a more competent dog at the helm.

Our domestic dogs still measure themselves against other members of their group—us! Dog owners whose actions lead to positive results have willing, secure followers. But dogs may step up and fill the void or cut loose and do their own thing when their people fail to show capable leadership. When dogs are pushy, aggressive, and rude, or independent and unwilling, it's not because they have designs on the role of "master." It is more likely that their owners failed to provide consistent leadership.

Dogs in training benefit from their handler's good leadership. Their education flows smoothly because they are impressed. Being in charge doesn't require you to physically dominate or punish your dog. You simply need to make some subtle changes in the way you relate to him every day.

Lead Your Pack!

Create schedules and structure daily activities. Dogs are creatures of habit and routines will create security. Feed meals at the same times each day and also try to schedule regular walks, training practices, and toilet outings. Your predictability will help your dog be patient.

Ask your dog to perform a task. Before releasing him to food or freedom, have him do something as simple as sit on command. Teach him that cooperation earns great results!

Give a release prompt (such as "let's go") when going through doors leading outside. This is a better idea than allowing your impatient pup to rush past you.

Pet your dog when he is calm, not when he is excited. Turn your touch into a tool that relaxes and settles.

Reward desirable rather than inappropriate behavior. Petting a jumping dog (who hasn't been invited up) reinforces jumping. Pet sitting dogs, and only invite lap dogs up after they've first "asked" by waiting for your invitation.

Replace personal punishment with positive reinforcement. Show a dog what *to do,* and motivate him to want to do it, and there will be no need to punish him for what he should *not do.* Dogs naturally follow, without the need for force or harshness.

Play creatively and appropriately. Your dog will learn the most about his social rank when he is playing with you. During play, dogs work to control toys and try to get the best of one another in a friendly way. The wrong sorts of play can create problems: For example, tug of war can lead to aggressiveness. Allowing your dog to control toys during play may result in possessive guarding when he has something he really values, such as a bone. Dogs who are chased during play may later run away from you when you approach to leash them. The right kinds of play will help increase your dog's social confidence while you gently assert your leadership.

How Dogs Learn (And How They Don't)

Dog training begins as a meeting of minds—yours and your dog's. Though the end goal may be to get your dog's body to behave in a specific way, training starts as a mind game. Your dog is learning all the time by observing the consequences of his actions and social interactions. He is always seeking out what he perceives as desirable and trying to avoid what he perceives as undesirable.

He will naturally repeat a behavior that either brings him more good stuff or makes bad stuff go away (these are both types of reinforcement). He will naturally avoid a behavior that brings him more bad stuff or makes the good stuff go away (these are both types of punishment).

Both reinforcement and punishment can be perceived as either the direct result of something the dog did himself, or as coming from an outside source.

Using Life's Rewards

Your best friend is smart, and he is also cooperative. When the best things in life can only be had by working with you, your dog will view you as a facilitator. You unlock doors to all of the positively reinforcing experiences he values: his freedom, his friends at the park, food, affection, walks, and play. The trained dog accompanies you through those doors and waits to see what working with you will bring.

Rewarding your dog for good behavior is called positive reinforcement, and, as we've just seen, it increases the likelihood that he will repeat that behavior. The perfect reward is anything your dog wants that is safe and appropriate. Don't limit yourself to toys, treats, and things that come directly from you. Harness life's positives—barking at squirrels, chasing a falling leaf, bounding away from you at the dog park, pausing for a moment to sniff everything—and allow your dog to earn access to those things as rewards that come from cooperating with you. When he looks at you, when he sits, when he comes when you call—any prompted behavior can earn one of life's rewards. When he works with you, he earns the things he most appreciates; but when he tries to get those things on his own, he cannot. Rather than see you as someone who always says "no," your dog will view you as the one who says "let's go!" He will *want* to follow.

What About Punishment?

Not only is it unnecessary to personally punish dogs, it is abusive. No matter how convinced you are that your dog "knows right from wrong," in reality he will associate personal punishment with the punisher. The resulting cowering, "guilty"-looking postures are actually displays of submission and fear. Later,

Purely Positive Reinforcement

With positive training, we emphasize teaching dogs what they should do to earn reinforcements, rather than punishing them for unwanted behaviors.

- Focus on teaching "do" rather than "don't." For example, a sitting dog isn't jumping.
- Use positive reinforcers that are valuable to your dog and the situation: A tired dog values rest; a confined dog values freedom.
- Play (appropriately)!
- Be a consistent leader.
- Set your dog up for success by anticipating and preventing problems.
- Notice and reward desirable behavior, and give him lots of attention when he is being good.
- Train ethically. Use humane methods and equipment that do not frighten or hurt your dog.
- When you are angry, walk away and plan a positive strategy.
- Keep practice sessions short and sweet. Five to ten minutes, three to five times a day is best.

when the punisher isn't around and the coast is clear, the same behavior he was punished for—such as raiding a trash can—might bring a self-delivered, very tasty result. The punished dog hasn't learned not to misbehave; he has learned to not get caught.

Does punishment ever have a place in dog training? Many people will heartily insist it does not. But dog owners often get frustrated as they try to stick to the path of all-positive reinforcement. It sure sounds great, but is it realistic, or even natural, to *never* say "no" to your dog?

A wild dog's life is not *all* positive. Hunger and thirst are both examples of negative reinforcement; the resulting discomfort motivates the wild dog to seek food and water. He encounters natural aversives such as pesky insects; mats in his coat; cold days; rainy days; sweltering hot days; and occasional run-ins with thorns, brambles, skunks, bees, and other nastiness. These all affect his behavior, as he tries to avoid the bad stuff whenever possible. The wild dog also occasionally encounters social punishers from others in his group when he gets too pushy. Starting with a growl or a snap from Mom, and later some mild and ritualized discipline from other members of his four-legged family, he learns to modify behaviors that elicit grouchy responses.

Our pet dogs don't naturally experience all positive results either, because they learn from their surroundings and from social experiences with other dogs. Watch a group of pet dogs playing together and you'll see a very old educational system still being used. As they wrestle and attempt to assert themselves, you'll notice many mouth-on-neck moments. Their playful biting is inhibited, with no intention to cause harm, but their message is clear: "Say uncle or this could hurt more!"

Observing that punishment does occur in nature, some people may feel compelled to try to be like the big wolf with their pet dogs. Becoming aggressive or heavy-handed with your pet will backfire! Your dog will not be impressed, nor will he want to follow you. Punishment causes dogs to change their behavior to avoid or escape discomfort and threats. Threatened dogs will either become very passive and offer submissive, appeasing postures, attempt to flee, or rise to the occasion and fight back. When people personally punish their dogs in an angry manner, one of these three defensive mechanisms will be triggered. Which one depends on a dog's genetic temperament as well as his past social experiences. Since we don't want to make our pets feel the need to avoid or escape us, personal punishment has no place in our training.

Remote Consequences

Sometimes, however, all-positive reinforcement is just not enough. That's because not all reinforcement comes from us. An inappropriate behavior can be self-reinforcing—just doing it makes the dog feel better in some way, whether you are there to say "good boy!" or not. Some examples are eating garbage, pulling the stuffing out of your sofa, barking at passersby, or urinating on the floor.

Although you don't want to personally punish your dog, the occasional deterrent may be called for to help derail these kinds of self-rewarding misbehaviors. In these cases, mild forms of impersonal or remote punishment can be used as part of a correction. The goal isn't to make your dog feel bad or to "know he has done wrong," but to help redirect him to alternate behaviors that are more acceptable to you.

The Problems with Personal Punishment

- Personally punished dogs are not taught appropriate behaviors.
- Personally punished dogs only stop misbehaving when they are caught or interrupted, but they don't learn not to misbehave when they are alone.
- Personally punished dogs become shy, fearful, and distrusting.
- Personally punished dogs may become defensively aggressive.
- Personally punished dogs become suppressed and inhibited.
- Personally punished dogs become stressed, triggering stress-reducing behaviors that their owners interpret as acts of spite, triggering even more punishment.
- Personally punished dogs have stressed owners.
- Personally punished dogs may begin to repeat behaviors they have been taught will result in negative, but predictable, attention.
- Personally punished dogs are more likely to be given away than are positively trained dogs.

You do this by pairing a slightly startling, totally impersonal sound with an equally impersonal and *very mild* remote consequence. The impersonal sound might be a single shake of an empty plastic pop bottle with pennies in it, held out of your dog's sight. Or you could use a vocal expression such as "eh!" delivered with you looking *away* from your misbehaving dog.

Pair your chosen sound—the penny bottle or "eh!"—with either a slight tug on his collar or a sneaky spritz on the rump from a water bottle. Do this right *as* he touches something he should not; bad timing will confuse your dog and undermine your training success.

To keep things under your control and make sure you get the timing right, it's best to do this as a setup. "Accidentally" drop a shoe on the floor, and then help your dog learn some things are best avoided. As he sniffs the shoe say "eh!" without looking at him and give a *slight* tug against his collar. This sound will quickly become meaningful as a correction all by itself—sometimes after just one setup—making the tug correction obsolete. The tug lets your dog see that you were right; going for that shoe *was* a bad idea! Your wise dog will be more likely to heed your warning next time, and probably move closer to you where it's safe. Be a good friend and pick up the nasty shoe. He'll be relieved, and you'll look heroic. Later, when he's home alone and encounters a stray shoe, he'll want to give it a wide berth.

Your negative marking sound will come in handy in the future, when your dog begins to venture down the wrong behavioral path. The goal is not to announce your disapproval or to threaten your dog. You are not telling him to stop or showing how *you* feel about his behavior. You are sounding a warning to a friend who's venturing off toward danger—"I wouldn't if I were you!" Suddenly, there is an abrupt, rather startling, noise! Now is the moment to redirect him and help him earn positive reinforcement. That interrupted behavior will become something he wants to avoid in the future, but he won't want to avoid you.

Practical Commands for Family Pets

Before you begin training your dog, let's look at some equipment you'll want to have on hand:

- **A buckle collar** is fine for most dogs. If your dog pulls *very* hard, try a head collar, a device similar to a horse halter that helps reduce pulling by turning the dog's head. *Do not* use a choke chain (sometimes called a training collar), because they cause physical harm even when used correctly.
- **Six-foot training leash and twenty-six–foot retractable leash.**
- **A few empty plastic soda bottles with about twenty pennies in each one.** This will be used to impersonally interrupt misbehaviors before redirecting dogs to more positive activities.
- **A favorite squeaky toy,** to motivate, attract attention, and reward your dog during training.

Lure your dog to take just a few steps with you on the leash by being inviting and enthusiastic. Make sure you reward him for his efforts.

Baby Steps

Allow your young pup to drag a short, lightweight leash attached to a buckle collar for a few *supervised* moments, several times each day. At first the leash may annoy him, and he may jump around a bit trying to get away from it. Distract him with your squeaky toy or a bit of his kibble and he'll quickly get used to his new "tail."

Begin walking him on the leash by holding the end and following him. As he adapts, you can begin to assert gentle direct pressure to teach him to follow you. Don't jerk or yank, or he will become afraid to walk when the leash is on. If he becomes hesitant, squat down facing him and let him figure out that by moving toward you, he is safe and secure. If he remains confused or frightened and doesn't come to you, go to him and help him understand that you provide safe harbor while he's on the leash. Then back away a few steps and try again to lure him to you. As he learns that you are the "home base," he'll want to follow when you walk a few steps, waiting for you to stop, squat down, and make him feel great.

So Attached to You!

The next step in training your dog—and this is a very important one—is to begin spending at least an hour or more each day with him on a four- to six-foot leash, held by or tethered to you. This training will increase his attachment to you—literally!—as you sit quietly or walk about, tending to your household business. When you are quiet, he'll learn it is time to settle; when you are active, he'll learn to move with you. Tethering also keeps him out of trouble when you are busy but still want his company. It is a great alternative to confining a dog, and can be used instead of crating any time you're home and need to slow him down a bit.

Rotating your dog from supervised freedom to tethered time to some quiet time in the crate or his gated area gives him a diverse and balanced day while he is learning. Two confined or tethered hours is the most you should require of your dog in one stretch, before changing to some supervised freedom, play, or a walk.

The dog in training may, at times, be stressed by all of the changes he is dealing with. Provide a stress outlet, such as a toy to chew on, when he is confined or tethered. He will settle into his quiet time more quickly and completely. Always be sure to provide several rounds of daily play and free time (in a fenced area or on your retractable leash) in addition to plenty of chewing materials.

Tethering your dog is a great way to keep him calm and under control, but still with you.

Dog Talk

Dogs don't speak in words, but they do have a language—body language. They use postures, vocalizations, movements, facial gestures, odors, and touch—usually with their mouths—to communicate what they are feeling and thinking.

We also "speak" using body language. We have quite an array of postures, movements, and facial gestures that accompany our touch and language as we attempt to communicate with our pets. And our dogs can quickly figure us out!

Alone, without associations, words are just noises. But, because we pair them with meaningful body language, our dogs make the connection. Dogs can really learn to understand much of what we *say*, if what we *do* at the same time is consistent.

The Positive Marker

Start your dog's education with one of the best tricks in dog training: Pair various positive reinforcers—food, a toy, touch—with a sound such as a click on a clicker (which you can get at the pet supply store) or a spoken word like "good!" or "yes!" This will enable you to later "mark" your dog's desirable behaviors.

It seems too easy: Just say "yes!" and give the dog his toy. (Or use whatever sound and reward you have chosen.) Later, when you make your marking sound right at the instant your dog does the right thing, he will know you are going to be giving him something good for that particular action. And he'll be eager to repeat the behavior to hear you mark it again!

Next, you must teach your dog to understand the meaning of cues you'll be using to ask him to perform specific behaviors. This is easy, too. Does he already do things you might like him to do on command? Of course! He lies down, he sits, he picks things up, he drops them again, he comes to you. All of the behaviors you'd like to control are already part of your dog's natural repertoire. The trick is getting him to offer those behaviors when you ask for them. And that means you have to teach him to associate a particular behavior on his part with a particular behavior on your part.

Sit Happens

Teach your dog an important new rule: From now on, he is only touched and petted when he is either sitting or lying down. You won't need to ask him to sit; in fact, you should not. Just keeping him tethered near you so there isn't much to do but stand, be ignored, or settle, and wait until sit happens.

He may pester you a bit, but be stoic and unresponsive. Starting now, when *you* are sitting down, a sitting dog is the only one you see and pay attention to. He will eventually sit, and as he does, attach the word "sit"—but don't be too excited or he'll jump right back up. Now mark with your positive sound that promises something good, then reward him with a slow, quiet, settling pet.

Training requires consistent reinforcement. Ask others to also wait until your dog is sitting and calm to touch him, and he will associate being petted with being relaxed. Be sure you train your dog to associate everyone's touch with quiet bonding.

Reinforcing "Sit" as a Command

Since your dog now understands one concept of working for a living—sit to earn petting—you can begin to shape and reinforce his desire to sit. Hold toys, treats, his bowl of food, and turn into a statue. But don't prompt him to sit! Instead, remain frozen and unavailable, looking somewhere out into space, over his head. He will put on a bit of a show, trying to get a response from you, and may offer various behaviors, but only one will push your button—sitting. Wait for him to offer the "right" behavior, and when he does, you unfreeze. Say "sit," then mark with an excited "good!" and give him the toy or treat with a release command—"OK!"

When you notice spontaneous sits occurring, be sure to take advantage of those free opportunities to make your command sequence meaningful and positive. Say "sit" as you observe sit happen—then mark with "good!" and praise, pet, or reward the dog. Soon, every time you look at your dog, he'll be sitting and looking right back at you!

Now, after thirty days of purely positive practice, it's time to give him a test. When he is just walking around doing his own thing, suddenly ask him to sit. He'll probably do it right away. If he doesn't, do *not* repeat your command, or you'll just undermine its meaning ("sit" means sit *now;* the command is not "sit, sit, sit, sit"). Instead, get something he likes and let him know you have it. Wait for him to offer the sit—he will—then say "sit!" and complete your marking and rewarding sequence.

OK

"OK" will probably rate as one of your dog's favorite words. It's like the word "recess" to schoolchildren. It is the word used to release your dog from a command. You can introduce "OK" during your "sit" practice. When he gets up from a sit, say "OK" to tell him the sitting is finished. Soon that sound will mean "freedom."

Make it even more meaningful and positive. Whenever he spontaneously bounds away, say "OK!" Squeak a toy, and when he notices and shows interest, toss it for him.

Down

I've mentioned that you should pet your dog only when he is either sitting or lying down. Now, using the approach I've just introduced for "sit," teach your dog to lie down. You will be a statue, and hold something he would like to get but that you'll release only to a dog who is lying down. It helps to lower the desired item to the floor in front of him, still not speaking and not letting him have it until he offers you the new behavior you are seeking.

Lower your dog's reward to the floor to help him figure out what behavior will earn him his reward.

He may offer a sit and then wait expectantly, but you must make him keep searching for the new trick that triggers your generosity. Allow your dog to experiment and find the right answer, even if he has to search around for it first. When he lands on "down" and learns it is another behavior that works, he'll offer it more quickly the next time.

Don't say "down" until he lies down, to tightly associate your prompt with the correct behavior. To say "down, down, down" as he is sitting, looking at you, or pawing at the toy would make "down" mean those behaviors instead! Whichever behavior he offers, a training opportunity has been created. Once you've attached and shaped both sitting and lying down, you can ask for both behaviors with your verbal prompts, "sit" or "down." Be sure to only reinforce the "correct" reply!

Stay

"Stay" can easily be taught as an extension of what you've already been practicing. To teach "stay," you follow the entire sequence for reinforcing a "sit" or "down," except you wait a bit longer before you give the release word, "OK!" Wait a second or two longer during each practice before saying "OK!" and releasing your dog to the positive reinforcer (toy, treat, or one of life's other rewards).

You can step on the leash to help your dog understand the down-stay, but only do this when he is already lying down. You don't want to hurt him!

If he gets up before you've said "OK," you have two choices: pretend the release was your idea and quickly interject "OK!" as he breaks; or, if he is more experienced and practiced, mark the behavior with your correction sound— "eh!"— and then gently put him back on the spot, wait for him to lie down, and begin again. Be sure the next three practices are a success. Ask him to wait for just a second, and release him before he can be wrong. You need to keep your dog feeling like more of a success than a failure as you begin to test his training in increasingly more distracting and difficult situations.

As he gets the hang of it—he stays until you say "OK"— you can gradually push for longer times—up to a minute on a sit-stay, and up to three minutes on a down-stay. You can also gradually add distractions and work in new environments. To add a minor self-correction for the down-stay, stand on the dog's leash after he lies down, allowing about three inches of slack. If he tries to get up before you've said "OK," he'll discover it doesn't work.

Do not step on the leash to make your dog lie down! This could badly hurt his neck, and will destroy his trust in you. Remember, we are teaching our dogs to make the best choices, not inflicting our answers upon them!

Come

Rather than think of "come" as an action—"come to me"—think of it as a place—"the dog is sitting in front of me, facing me." Since your dog by now really likes sitting to earn your touch and other positive reinforcement, he's likely to sometimes sit directly in front of you, facing you, all on his own. When this happens, give it a specific name: "come."

Now follow the rest of the training steps you have learned to make him like doing it and reinforce the behavior by practicing it any chance you get. Anything your dog wants and likes could be earned as a result of his first offering the sit-in-front known as "come."

You can help guide him into the right location. Use your hands as "landing gear" and pat the insides of your legs at his nose level. Do this while backing up a bit, to help him maneuver to the straight-in-front, facing-you position. Don't say the

Pat the insides of your legs to show your dog exactly where you like him to sit when you say "come."

word "come" while he's maneuvering, because he hasn't! You are trying to make "come" the end result, not the work in progress.

You can also help your dog by marking his movement in the right direction: Use your positive sound or word to promise he is getting warm. When he finally sits facing you, enthusiastically say "come," mark again with your positive word, and release him with an enthusiastic "OK!" Make it so worth his while, with lots of play and praise, that he can't wait for you to ask him to come again!

Building a Better Recall

Practice, practice, practice. Now, practice some more. Teach your dog that all good things in life hinge upon him first sitting in front of you in a behavior named "come." When you think he really has got it, test him by asking him to "come" as you gradually add distractions and change locations. Expect setbacks as you make these changes and practice accordingly. Lower your expectations and make his task easier so he is able to get it right. Use those distractions as rewards, when they are appropriate. For example, let him check out the interesting leaf that blew by as a reward for first coming to you and ignoring it.

Add distance and call your dog to come while he is on his retractable leash. If he refuses and sits looking at you blankly, *do not* jerk, tug, "pop," or reel him in. Do nothing! It is his move; wait to see what behavior he offers. He'll either begin to approach (mark the behavior with an excited "good!"), sit and do nothing (just keep waiting), or he'll try to move in some direction other than toward you. If he tries to leave, use your correction marker—"eh!"— and bring him to a stop by letting him walk to the end of the leash, *not* by jerking him. Now walk to him in a neutral manner, and don't jerk or show any disapproval. Gently bring him back to the spot where he was when you called him, then back away and face him, still waiting and not reissuing your command. Let him keep examining his options until he finds the one that works—yours!

If you have practiced everything I've suggested so far and given your dog a chance to really learn what "come" means, he is well aware of what you want and is quite intelligently weighing all his options. The only way he'll know your way is the one that works is to be allowed to examine his other choices and discover that they *don't* work.

Sooner or later every dog tests his training. Don't be offended or angry when your dog tests you. No matter how positive you've made it, he won't always want to do everything you ask, every time. When he explores the "what happens if I don't" scenario, your training is being strengthened. He will discover through his own process of trial and error that the best—and only—way out of a command he really doesn't feel compelled to obey is to obey it.

Let's Go

Many pet owners wonder if they can retain control while walking their dogs and still allow at least some running in front, sniffing, and playing. You might worry that allowing your dog occasional freedom could result in him expecting it all the time, leading to a testy, leash-straining walk. It's possible for both parties on the leash to have an enjoyable experience by implementing and reinforcing well-thought-out training techniques.

Begin by making word associations you'll use on your walks. Give the dog some slack on the leash, and as he starts to walk away from you say "OK" and begin to follow him.

Give your dog slack on his leash as you walk and let him make the decision to walk with you.

Do not let him drag you; set the pace even when he is being given a turn at being the leader. Whenever he starts to pull, just come to a standstill and refuse to move (or refuse to allow him to continue forward) until there is slack in the leash. Do this correction without saying anything at all. When he isn't pulling, you may decide to just stand still and let him sniff about within the range the slack leash allows, or you may even mosey along following him. After a few minutes of "recess," it is time to work. Say something like "that's it" or "time's up," close the distance between you and your dog, and touch him.

Next say "let's go" (or whatever command you want to use to mean "follow me as we walk"). Turn and walk off, and, if he follows, mark his behavior with "good!" Then stop,

When your dog catches up with you, make sure you let him know what a great dog he is!

Intersperse periods of attentive walking, where your dog is on a shorter leash, with periods on a slack leash, where he is allowed to look and sniff around.

squat down, and let him catch you. Make him glad he did! Start again, and do a few transitions as he gets the hang of your follow-the-leader game, speeding up, slowing down, and trying to make it fun. When you stop, he gets to catch up and receive some deserved positive reinforcement. Don't forget that's the reason he is following you, so be sure to make it worth his while!

Require him to remain attentive to you. Do not allow sniffing, playing, eliminating, or pulling during your time as leader on a walk. If he seems to get distracted—which, by the way, is the main reason dogs walk poorly with their people— change direction or pace without saying a word. Just help him realize "oops, I lost track of my human." Do not jerk his neck and say "heel"—this will make the word "heel" mean pain in the neck and will not encourage him to cooperate with you. Don't repeat "let's go," either. He needs to figure out that it is his job to keep track of and follow you if he wants to earn the positive benefits you provide.

The best reward you can give a dog for performing an attentive, controlled walk is a few minutes of walking without all of the controls. Of course, he must remain on a leash even during the "recess" parts of the walk, but allowing him to discriminate between attentive following—"let's go"—and having a few moments of relaxation—"OK"—will increase his willingness to work.

Training for Attention

Your dog pretty much has a one-track mind. Once he is focused on something, everything else is excluded. This can be great, for instance, when he's focusing on you! But it can also be dangerous if, for example, his attention is riveted on the bunny he is chasing and he does not hear you call—that is, not unless he has been trained to pay attention when you say his name.

When you say your dog's name, you'll want him to make eye contact with you. Begin teaching this by making yourself so intriguing that he can't help but look.

When you call your dog's name, you will again be seeking a specific response—eye contact. The best way to teach this is to trigger his alerting response by making a noise with your mouth, such as whistling or a kissing sound, and then immediately doing something he'll find very intriguing.

You can play a treasure hunt game to help teach him to regard his name as a request for attention. As a bonus, you can reinforce the rest of his new vocabulary at the same time.

Treasure Hunt

Make a kissing sound, then jump up and find a dog toy or dramatically raid the fridge and rather noisily eat a piece of cheese. After doing this twice, make a kissing sound and then look at your dog.

Of course he is looking at you! He is waiting to see if that sound—the kissing sound—means you're going to go hunting again. After all, you're so good at it! Because he is looking, say his name, mark with "good," then go hunting and find his toy. Release it to him with an "OK." At any point if he follows you, attach your "let's go!" command; if he leaves you, give permission with "OK."

Using this approach, he cannot be wrong—any behavior your dog offers can be named. You can add things like "take it" when he picks up a toy, and "thank you" when he happens to drop one. Many opportunities to make your new vocabulary meaningful and positive can be found within this simple training game.

Problems to watch out for when teaching the treasure hunt:

- You really do not want your dog to come to you when you call his name (later, when you try to engage his attention to ask him to stay, he'll already be on his way toward you). You just want him to look at you.
- Saying "watch me, watch me" doesn't teach your dog to *offer* his attention. It just makes you a background noise.
- Don't lure your dog's attention with the reward. Get his attention and then reward him for looking. Try holding a toy in one hand with your arm stretched out to your side. Wait until he looks at you rather than the toy. Now say his name then mark with "good!" and release the toy. As he goes for it, say "OK."

To get your dog's attention, try holding his toy with your arm out to your side. Wait until he looks at you, then mark the moment and give him the toy.

Teaching Cooperation

Never punish your dog for failing to obey you or try to punish him into compliance. Bribing, repeating yourself, and doing a behavior for him all avoid the real issue of dog training—his will. He must be helped to be willing, not made to achieve tasks. Good dog training helps your dog want to obey. He learns that he can gain what he values most through cooperation and compliance, and can't gain those things any other way.

Your dog is learning to *earn*, rather than expect, the good things in life. And you've become much more important to him than you were before. Because you are allowing him to experiment and learn, he doesn't have to be forced, manipulated, or bribed. When he wants something, he can gain it by cooperating with you. One of those "somethings"—and a great reward you shouldn't underestimate—is your positive attention, paid to him with love and sincere approval!

Chapter 10

Housetraining Your Labrador Retriever

Excerpted from Housetraining: An Owner's Guide to a Happy Healthy Pet, 1st Edition, *by September Morn*

By the time puppies are about 3 weeks old, they start to follow their mother around. When they are a few steps away from their clean sleeping area, the mama dog stops. The pups try to nurse but mom won't allow it. The pups mill around in frustration, then nature calls, and they all urinate and defecate here, away from their bed. The mother dog returns to the nest, with her brood waddling behind her. Their first housetraining lesson has been a success.

The next one to housetrain puppies should be their breeder. The breeder watches as the puppies eliminate, then deftly removes the soiled papers and replaces them with clean papers before the pups can traipse back through their messes. He has wisely arranged the puppies' space so their bed, food, and drinking water are as far away from the elimination area as possible. This way, when the pups follow their mama, they will move away from their sleeping and eating area before eliminating. This habit will help the pups be easily housetrained.

Your Housetraining Shopping List

While your puppy's mother and breeder are getting her started on good house-training habits, you'll need to do some shopping. If you have all the essentials in place before your dog arrives, it will be easier to help her learn the rules from day one.

Newspaper: The younger your puppy and larger her breed, the more newspapers you'll need. Newspaper is absorbent, abundant, cheap, and convenient.

Puddle Pads: If you prefer not to stockpile newspaper, a commercial alternative is puddle pads. These thick paper pads can be purchased under several trade names at pet supply stores. The pads have waterproof backing, so puppy urine doesn't seep through onto the floor. Their disadvantages are that they will cost you more than newspapers and that they contain plastics that are not biodegradable.

Poop Removal Tool: There are several types of poop removal tools available. Some are designed with a separate pan and rake, and others have the handles hinged like scissors. Some scoops need two hands for operation, while others are designed for one-handed use. Try out the different brands at your pet supply store. Put a handful of pebbles or dog kibble on the floor and then pick them up with each type of scoop to determine which works best for you.

Plastic Bags: When you take your dog outside your yard, you *must* pick up after her. Dog waste is unsightly, smelly, and can harbor disease. In many cities and towns, the law mandates that dog owners clean up pet waste deposited on public ground. Picking up after your dog using a plastic bag scoop is simple. Just put your hand inside the bag, like a mitten, and then grab the droppings. Turn the bag inside out, tie the top, and that's that.

Crate: To housetrain a puppy, you will need some way to confine her when you're unable to supervise. A dog crate is a secure way to confine your dog for short periods during the day and to use as a comfortable bed at night. Crates come in wire mesh and in plastic. The wire ones are foldable to store flat in a smaller space. The plastic ones are more cozy, draft-free, and quiet, and are approved for airline travel.

Baby Gates: Since you shouldn't crate a dog for more than an hour or two at a time during the day, baby gates are a good way to limit your dog's freedom in the house. Be sure the baby gates you use are safe. The old-fashioned wooden, expanding lattice type has seriously injured a number of children by collapsing and trapping a leg, arm, or neck. That type of gate can hurt a puppy, too, so use the modern grid type gates instead. You'll need more than one baby gate if you have several doorways to close off.

Exercise Pen: Portable exercise pens are great when you have a young pup or a small dog. These metal or plastic pens are made of rectangular panels that are hinged together. The pens are freestanding, sturdy, foldable, and can be carried like a suitcase. You could set one up in your kitchen as the pup's daytime corral, and then take it outdoors to contain your pup while you garden or just sit and enjoy the day.

Enzymatic Cleaner: All dogs make housetraining mistakes. Accept this and be ready for it by buying an enzymatic cleaner made especially for pet accidents. Dogs like to eliminate where they have done it before, and lingering smells lead them to those spots. Ordinary household cleaners may remove all the odors you can smell, but only an enzymatic cleaner will remove everything your dog can smell.

The First Day

Housetraining is a matter of establishing good habits in your dog. That means you never want her to learn anything she will eventually have to unlearn. Start off housetraining on the right foot by teaching your dog that you prefer her to eliminate outside. Designate a potty area in your backyard (if you have one) or in the street in front of your home and take your dog to it as soon as you arrive home. Let her sniff a bit and, when she squats to go, give the action a name: "potty" or "do it" or anything else you won't be embarrassed to say in public. Eventually your dog will associate that word with the act and will eliminate on command. When she's finished, praise her with "good potty!"

That first day, take your puppy out to the potty area frequently. Although she may not eliminate every time, you are establishing a routine: You take her to her spot, ask her to eliminate, and praise her when she does.

Just before bedtime, take your dog to her potty area once more. Stand by and wait until she produces. Do not put your dog to bed for the night until she has eliminated. Be patient and calm. This is not the time to play with or excite your

Take your pup out frequently to her special potty spot and praise her when she goes.

dog. If she's too excited, a pup not only won't eliminate, she probably won't want to sleep either.

Most dogs, even young ones, will not soil their beds if they can avoid it. For this reason, a sleeping crate can be a tremendous help during housetraining. Being crated at night can help a dog develop the muscles that control elimination. So after your dog has emptied out, put her to bed in her crate.

A good place to put your dog's sleeping crate is near your own bed. Dogs are pack animals, so they feel safer sleeping with others in a common area. In your bedroom, the pup will be near you, and you'll be close enough to hear when she wakes during the night and needs to eliminate.

Pups under 4 months old often are not able to hold their urine all night. If your puppy has settled down to sleep but awakens and fusses a few hours later, she probably needs to go out. For the best housetraining progress, take your pup to her elimination area whenever she needs to go, even in the wee hours of the morning.

Your pup may soil in her crate if you ignore her late night urgency. It's unfair to let this happen, and it sends the wrong message about your expectations for

Your dog's crate is a great housetraining tool.

cleanliness. Resign yourself to this midnight outing and just get up and take the pup out. Your pup will outgrow this need soon and will learn in the process that she can count on you, and you'll wake happily each morning to a clean dog.

The next morning, the very first order of business is to take your pup out to eliminate. Don't forget to take her to her special potty spot, ask her to eliminate, and then praise her when she does. After your pup empties out in the morning, give her breakfast, and then take her to her potty area again. After that, she shouldn't need to eliminate again right away, so you can allow her some free playtime. Keep an eye on the pup though, because when she pauses in play she may need to go potty. Take her to the right spot, give the command, and praise if she produces.

Confine Your Pup

A pup or dog who has not finished housetraining should *never* be allowed the run of the house unattended. A new dog (especially a puppy) with unlimited access to your house will make her own choices about where to eliminate. Vigilance during your new dog's first few weeks in your home will pay big dividends. Every potty mistake delays housetraining progress; every success speeds it along.

Prevent problems by setting up a controlled environment for your new pet. A good place for a puppy corral is often the kitchen. Kitchens almost always have waterproof or easily cleaned floors, which is a distinct asset with leaky pups. A bathroom, laundry room, or enclosed porch could be used for a puppy corral, but the kitchen is generally the best location. Kitchens are a meeting place and a hub of activity for many families, and a puppy will learn better manners when she is socialized thoroughly with family, friends, and nice strangers.

The way you structure your pup's corral area is very important. Her bed, food, and water should be at the opposite end of the corral from the potty area. When you first get your pup, spread newspaper over the rest of the floor of her playpen corral. Lay the papers at least four pages thick and be sure to overlap the edges. As you note the pup's progress, you can remove the papers nearest the sleeping and eating corner. Gradually decrease the size of the papered area until only the end where you want the pup to eliminate is covered. If you will be training your dog to eliminate outside, place newspaper at the end of the corral that is closest to the door that leads outdoors. That way as she moves away from the clean area to the papered area, the pup will also form the habit of heading toward the door to go out.

Maintain a scent marker for the pup's potty area by reserving a small soiled piece of paper when you clean up. Place this piece, with her scent of urine, under the top sheet of the clean papers you spread. This will cue your pup where to eliminate.

Most dog owners use a combination of indoor papers and outdoor elimination areas. When the pup is left by herself in the corral, she can potty on the ever-present newspaper. When you are available to take the pup outside, she can do her business in the outdoor spot. It is not difficult to switch a pup from indoor paper training to outdoor elimination. Owners of large pups often switch early, but potty papers are still useful if the pup spends time in her indoor corral while you're away. Use the papers as long as your pup needs them. If you come home and they haven't been soiled, you are ahead.

Most dog owners use a combination of indoor paper and outdoor potty areas for housetraining. The kitchen is a good place to confine a pup for paper training.

Don't Overuse the Crate

A crate serves well as a dog's overnight bed, but you should not leave the dog in her crate for more than an hour or two during the day. Throughout the day, she needs to play and exercise. She is likely to want to drink some water and will undoubtedly eliminate. Confining your dog all day will give her no option but to soil her crate. This is not just unpleasant for you and the dog, but it reinforces bad cleanliness habits. And crating a pup for the whole day is abusive. Don't do it.

When you take your dog outside for a potty trip, don't play until after she's done. You don't want to distract her or confuse her about what this trip is for.

When setting up your pup's outdoor yard, put the lounging area as far away as possible from the potty area, just as with the indoor corral setup. People with large yards, for example, might leave a patch unmowed at the edge of the lawn to serve as the dog's elimination area. Other dog owners teach the dog to relieve herself in a designated corner of a deck or patio. For an apartment-dwelling city dog, the outdoor potty area might be a tiny balcony or the curb. Each dog owner has somewhat different expectations for their dog. Teach your dog to eliminate in a spot that suits your environment and lifestyle.

Be sure to pick up droppings in your yard at least once a day. Dogs have a natural desire to stay far away from their own excrement, and if too many piles litter the ground, your dog won't want to walk through it and will start eliminating elsewhere. Leave just one small piece of feces in the potty area to remind your dog where the right spot is located.

To help a pup adapt to the change from indoors to outdoors, take one of her potty papers outside to the new elimination area. Let the pup stand on the paper when she goes potty outdoors. Each day for four days, reduce the size of the paper by half. By the fifth day, the pup, having used a smaller and smaller piece of paper to stand on, will probably just go to that spot and eliminate.

Take your pup to her outdoor potty place frequently throughout the day. A puppy can hold her urine for only about as many hours as her age in months, and will move her bowels as many times a day as she eats. So a 2-month-old pup will urinate about every two hours, while at 4 months she can manage about four hours between piddles. Pups vary somewhat in their rate of development, so this is not a hard and fast rule. It does, however, present a realistic idea of how long a pup can be left without access to a potty place. Past 4 months, her potty trips will be less frequent.

When you take the dog outdoors to her spot, keep her leashed so that she won't wander away. Stand quietly and let her sniff around in the designated area. If your pup starts to leave before she has eliminated, gently lead her back and remind her to go. If your pup sniffs at the spot, praise her calmly, say the command word, and just wait. If she produces, praise serenely, then give her time to sniff around a little more. She may not be finished, so give her time to go again before allowing her to play and explore her new home.

If you find yourself waiting more than five minutes for your dog to potty, take her back inside. Watch your pup carefully for twenty minutes, not giving her any opportunity to slip away to eliminate unnoticed. If you are too busy to watch the pup, put her in her crate. After twenty minutes, take her to the outdoor potty spot again and tell her what to do. If you're unsuccessful after five minutes, crate the dog again. Give her another chance to eliminate in fifteen or twenty minutes. Eventually, she will have to go.

> **T I P**
>
> **Water**
>
> Make sure your dog has access to clean water at all times. Limiting the amount of water a dog drinks is not necessary for housetraining success and can be very dangerous. A dog needs water to digest food, to maintain a proper body temperature and proper blood volume, and to clean her system of toxins and wastes. A healthy dog will automatically drink the right amount. Do not restrict water intake. Controlling your dog's access to water is not the key to housetraining her; controlling her access to everything else in your home is.

Watch Your Pup

Be vigilant and don't let the pup make a mistake in the house. Each time you successfully anticipate elimination and take your pup to the potty spot, you'll move a step closer to your goal. Stay aware of your puppy's needs. If you ignore the pup, she will make mistakes, and you'll be cleaning up more messes.

Keep a chart of your new dog's elimination behavior for the first three or four days. Jot down what times she eats, sleeps, and eliminates. After several days a pattern will emerge that can help you determine your pup's body rhythms. Most dogs tend to eliminate at fairly regular intervals. Once you know your new dog's natural rhythms, you'll be able to anticipate her needs and schedule appropriate potty outings.

Understanding the meanings of your dog's postures can also help you win the battle of the puddle. When your dog is getting ready to eliminate, she will display a specific set of postures. The sooner you can learn to read these signals, the cleaner your floor will stay.

A young puppy who feels the urge to eliminate may start to sniff the ground and walk in a circle. If the pup is very young, she may simply squat and go. All young puppies, male or female, squat to urinate. If you are house-training a pup under 4 months of age, regardless of sex, watch for the beginnings of a squat as the signal to rush the pup to the potty area.

If you see your puppy getting ready to eliminate, whisk her outside so she can do the right thing.

When a puppy is getting ready to defecate, she may run urgently back and forth or turn in a circle while sniffing or starting to squat. If defecation is imminent, the pup's anus may protrude or open slightly. When she starts to go, the pup will squat and hunch her back, her tail sticking straight out behind. There is no mistaking this posture; nothing else looks like this. If your pup takes this position, take her to her potty area. Hurry! You may have to carry her to get there in time.

A young puppy won't have much time between feeling the urge and actually eliminating, so you'll have to be quick to note her postural clues and intercept your pup in time. Pups from 3 to 6 months have a few seconds more between the urge and the act than younger ones do. The older your pup, the more time you'll have to get her to the potty area after she begins the posture signals that alert you to her need.

Accidents Happen

If you see your pup about to eliminate somewhere other than the designated area, interrupt her immediately. Say "wait, wait, wait!" or clap your hands loudly to startle her into stopping. Carry the pup, if she's still small enough, or take her collar and lead her to the correct area. Once your dog is in the potty area, give her the command to eliminate. Use a friendly voice for the command, then wait patiently for her to produce. The pup may be tense because you've just startled her and may have to relax a bit before she's able to eliminate. When she does her job, include the command word in the praise you give ("good potty").

The old-fashioned way of housetraining involved punishing a dog's mistakes even before she knew what she was supposed to do. Puppies were punished for breaking rules they didn't understand about functions they couldn't control. This was not fair. While your dog is new to housetraining, there is no need or

It's not fair to expect your baby puppy to be able to control herself the way an adult dog can.

Housetraining is a huge task, but it doesn't go on forever. Be patient and eventually your puppy will be a reliable adult.

excuse for punishing her mistakes. Your job is to take the dog to the potty area just before she needs to go, especially with pups under 3 months old. If you aren't watching your pup closely enough and she has an accident, don't punish the puppy for your failure to anticipate her needs. It's not the pup's fault; it's yours.

In any case, punishment is not an effective tool for housetraining most dogs. Many will react to punishment by hiding puddles and feces where you won't find them right away (like behind the couch or under the desk). This eventually may lead to punishment after the fact, which leads to more hiding, and so on.

Instead of punishing for mistakes, stay a step ahead of potty accidents by learning to anticipate your pup's needs. Accompany your dog to the designated potty area when she needs to go. Tell her what you want her to do and praise her when she goes. This will work wonders. Punishment won't be necessary if you are a good teacher.

What happens if you come upon a mess after the fact? Some trainers say a dog can't remember having eliminated, even a few moments after she has done so. This is not true. The fact is that urine and feces carry a dog's unique scent, which she (and every other dog) can instantly recognize. So, if you happen upon a potty mistake after the fact you can still use it to teach your dog.

But remember, no punishment! Spanking, hitting, shaking, or scaring a puppy for having a housetraining accident is confusing and counterproductive. Spend your energy instead on positive forms of teaching.

Take your pup and a paper towel to the mess. Point to the urine or feces and calmly tell your puppy, "no potty here." Then scoop or sop up the accident with the paper towel. Take the evidence and the pup to the approved potty area. Drop the mess on the ground and tell the dog, "good potty here," as if she had done the deed in the right place. If your pup sniffs at the evidence, praise her calmly. If the accident happened very recently your dog may not have to go yet, but wait with her a few minutes anyway. If she eliminates, praise her. Afterwards, go finish cleaning up the mess.

Soon the puppy will understand that there is a place where you are pleased about elimination and other places where you are not. Praising for elimination in the approved place will help your pup remember the rules.

Scheduling Basics

With a new puppy in the home, don't be surprised if your rising time is suddenly a little earlier than you've been accustomed to. Puppies have earned a reputation as very early risers. When your pup wakes you at the crack of dawn, you will have to get up and take her to her elimination spot. Be patient. When your dog is an adult, she may enjoy sleeping in as much as you do.

At the end of the chapter, you'll find a typical housetraining schedule for puppies aged 10 weeks to 6 months. (To find schedules for younger and older pups, and for adult dogs, visit this book's companion Web site.) It's fine to adjust the rising times when using this schedule, but you should not adjust the intervals between feedings and potty outings unless your pup's behavior justifies a change. Your puppy can only meet your expectations in housetraining if you help her learn the rules.

The schedule for puppies is devised with the assumption that someone will be home most of the time with the pup. That would be the best scenario, of course, but is not always possible. You may be able to ease the problems of a latchkey pup by having a neighbor or friend look in on the pup at noon and take her to eliminate. A better solution might be hiring a pet sitter to drop by midday. A professional pet sitter will be knowledgeable about companion animals and can give your pup high-quality care and socialization. Some can even help train your pup in both potty manners and basic obedience. Ask your veterinarian and your dog-owning friends to recommend a good pet sitter.

If you must leave your pup alone during her early housetraining period, be sure to cover the entire floor of her corral with thick layers of overlapping newspaper. If you come home to messes in the puppy corral, just clean them up. Be patient—she's still a baby.

Use this schedule (and the ones on the companion Web site) as a basic plan to help prevent housetraining accidents. Meanwhile, use your own powers of observation to discover how to best modify the basic schedule to fit your dog's unique needs. Each dog is an individual and will have her own rhythms, and each dog is reliable at a different age.

Schedule for Pups 10 Weeks to 6 Months

7:00 a.m.	Get up and take the puppy from her sleeping crate to her potty spot.
7:15	Clean up last night's messes, if any.
7:30	Food and fresh water.
7:45	Pick up the food bowl. Take the pup to her potty spot; wait and praise.
8:00	The pup plays around your feet while you have your breakfast.
9:00	Potty break (younger pups may not be able to wait this long).
9:15	Play and obedience practice.
10:00	Potty break.
10:15	The puppy is in her corral with safe toys to chew and play with.
11:30	Potty break (younger pups may not be able to wait this long).
11:45	Food and fresh water.
12:00 p.m.	Pick up the food bowl and take the pup to her potty spot.
12:15	The puppy is in her corral with safe toys to chew and play with.
1:00	Potty break (younger pups may not be able to wait this long).
1:15	Put the pup on a leash and take her around the house with you.
3:30	Potty break (younger pups may not be able to wait this long).
3:45	Put the pup in her corral with safe toys and chews for solitary play and/or a nap.
4:45	Potty break.
5:00	Food and fresh water.
5:15	Potty break.
5:30	The pup may play nearby (either leashed or in her corral) while you prepare your evening meal.

7:00	Potty break.
7:15	Leashed or closely watched, the pup may play and socialize with family and visitors.
9:15	Potty break (younger pups may not be able to wait this long).
10:45	Last chance to potty.
11:00	Put the pup to bed in her crate for the night.

Appendix

Learning More About Your Labrador Retriever

Some Good Books

About the Breed

Walton, Joel, and Eve Adamson, *Labrador Retrievers for Dummies*, Wiley Publishing, 2000.

Weiss, Lisa, and Emily Biegel, *The Labrador Retriever: The Dog That Does It All*, Howell Book House, 1999.

Wiles-Fone, Heather, *The Ultimate Labrador Retriever*, 2nd ed., Howell Book House, 2003.

About Health Care

Arden, Darlene, *The Angell Memorial Animal Hospital Book of Wellness and Preventive Care for Dogs*, McGraw-Hill, 2004.

Eldredge, Debra, DVM, Delbert Carlson, DVM, Liisa Carlson, DVM, and James Giffin, MD, *Dog Owner's Home Veterinary Handbook*, 4th ed., Howell Book House, 2007.

Jacobs, Jocelynn, DVM, *Performance Dog Nutrition*, Sno Shire Publications, 2005.

Messonnier, Shawn, DVM, *Eight Weeks to a Healthy Dog*, Rodale Books, 2003.

Volhard, Wendy, and Kerry Brown, DVM, *Holistic Guide for a Healthy Dog*, Howell Book House, 2000.

About Training

McCullough, Susan, *Housetraining for Dummies*, Wiley Publishing, 2002.
Palika, Liz, *All Dogs Need Some Training*, Howell Book House, 1997.
Palika, Liz, *The KISS Guide to Raising a Puppy*, Dorling Kindersley, 2002.
Smith, Cheryl, *The Rosetta Bone*, Howell Book House, 2004.

Dog Sports and Activities

Davis, Kathy Diamond, *Therapy Dogs*, 2nd ed., DogWise Publishing, 2002.
Jones, Robert F., *Upland Passage: A Field Dog's Education*, The Lyons Press, 2004.
Palika, Liz, *The Complete Idiot's Guide to Dog Tricks*, Alpha Books, 2005.
Quinn, Tom, *The Working Retrievers: The Classic Book for the Training, Care, and Handling of Retrievers for Hunting and Field Trials*, The Lyons Press, 2003.

Magazines

AKC Gazette
260 Madison Ave.
New York, NY 10016
www.akc.org/pubs/index.cfm

Bloodlines
100 East Kilgore Rd.
Kalamazoo, MI 49002
www.ukcdogs.com

Dog Fancy
P.O. Box 37185
Boone, IA 50037-0185
www.dogfancy.com

Dog World
P.O. Box 37185
Boone, IA 50037-0185
www.dogworldmag.com

Gun Dog
P.O. Box 420235
Palm Coast, FL 32142-0235
(800) 800-7724
www.gundogmag.com

The Retriever Journal
2779 Aero Park Dr.
Traverse City, MI 49686
(800) 447-7367
retrieverjournal.com

Clubs and Registries

The Labrador Retriever Club of America
Membership Information
24670 Schaupp Rd.
Klamath Falls, OR 97603
www.thelabradorclub.com

This is the national club for the breed; its Web site has a great deal of information, including upcoming shows and competitions. There are also many all-breed, individual breed, canine sport, and other special-interest dog clubs across the country. The registries listed here can help you find clubs in your area.

American Kennel Club
260 Madison Ave.
New York, NY 10016
(212) 696-8200
www.akc.org

Canadian Kennel Club
89 Skyway Ave.
Etobicoke, Ontario
Canada M9W 6R4
(800) 250-8040 or (416) 675-5511
www.ckc.ca

United Kennel Club
100 East Kilgore Rd.
Kalamazoo, MI 49002
(616) 343-9020
www.ukcdogs.com

On the Internet

All About Labs

Just Labradors
www.justlabradors.com
A community for Labrador Retriever dog owners and enthusiasts. Visitors submit articles, links, photos, videos, and all things Lab.

Working Our Labrador Retrievers
www.thelabradorclub.com/library/gazette200504.html
Information from the Labrador Retriever Club of America that emphasizes the importance of working show dogs.

Canine Health

American Veterinary Medical Association
www.avma.org
A wealth of information for dog owners, from disaster preparedness to both common and rare diseases affecting canines. There is also information on choosing the right dog and dog bite prevention.

Canine Health Information Center
www.caninehealthinfo.org
A centralized canine health database jointly sponsored by the American Kennel Club Canine Health Foundation and the Orthopedic Foundation for Animals.

Justamere Ranch: Health Problems in Labrador Retrievers
www.justamere.com/newsletter/problems.asp
Descriptions of most of the most common disorders and diseases found in Labs.

Dog Sports and Activities

Bird Dog & Retriever News
www.bird-dog-news.com
A huge online and print hunting dog magazine, with hundreds of archived articles.

Dog Patch
www.dogpatch.org
Information on many different dog sports and activities, including herding, agility, and Frisbee.

Dog Play
www.dog-play.com
More about dog sports and activities, including hiking, backpacking, therapy dog work, and much more.

Working Dogs
www.workingdogs.com
An Internet magazine for people who own or train working dogs of all kinds.

Working Retriever Central
www.working-retriever.com
All about buying working retrievers, training working retrievers, and much more.

Index

Photo Credits: